Guide to the Use of Books and Libraries

JEAN KEY GATES
District of Columbia Teachers College

GUIDE

TO

THE USE

OF

BOOKS

AND

LIBRARIES

McGraw-Hill Book Company, Inc.
NEW YORK   TORONTO   LONDON   SAN FRANCISCO

1962

GUIDE
TO THE USE
OF BOOKS
AND LIBRARIES

III

Library of Congress Catalog Card Number: 61–15910

To Sherwood

PREFACE

THE purpose of this book is to provide a brief but comprehensive treatment of books and libraries, with emphasis upon the many kinds of library materials, their organization and arrangement, and their usefulness for specific purposes. Particular attention is paid to college libraries and to ways of using them most effectively.

Since it is my belief and experience that effective use of the library has its beginning in an appreciation and understanding of books and of their importance in one's academic and personal life, I have emphasized (1) the historical development of each aspect of the book and the library, and (2) the usefulness of each type of library material for particular purposes.

The chapters are arranged in logical sequence, and if the reader follows straight through the text he should gain a full-length picture of the college library and a reasonably clear picture of any library. There is some repetition of ideas and information. This repetition is by design: each chapter, while it is a necessary part of the whole, has been planned to stand alone so that the instructor who has only a limited time in which to teach the use of the library can select the chapter or parts of chapters best suited to his requirements and purposes.

In this book emphasis is placed upon *how to use books* rather than upon *the number of titles* included. The selection of titles to illustrate the several kinds of library materials was based on a critical study of the basic reference materials in a number of selective and evaluative bibliographies including:

Winchell, Constance M. *Guide to Reference Books.* 7th ed. Chicago: American Library Association, 1951.

Winchell, Constance M. *Supplements, 1950–1952; 1953–1955; 1956– 1958.* Chicago: American Library Association, 1954–1960.

Shores, Louis. *Basic Reference Sources: An Introduction to Materials and Methods.* Chicago: American Library Association, 1954.

Southern Association of Colleges and Secondary Schools. Commission on Colleges and Universities. *The Classified List of Reference Books and Periodicals for College Libraries.* 3d ed. Atlanta, Ga.: Southern Association of Colleges and Secondary Schools, 1955.

Also included are materials which I have used and evaluated in my own college teaching and reference work. The titles listed are thus only a selected sample of those now available, and each person will undoubtedly wish to add titles of his own choosing and to replace, with new editions and new titles, some of those which have been included.

This book is not a manual for the study of a particular library. It is designed to serve as a textbook for college freshmen and other students who require instruction in the use of books and libraries. It will provide supplementary material for introductory courses in library science and can be used to advantage not only by reference librarians but by any person who is interested in learning what a library is and how to use it.

I am indebted to the authors, publishers, and holders of copyrights for their kind permission to use their material, and I want to give special credit to the works of Miss Constance M. Winchell (listed above), which were particularly useful to me in selecting the titles to illustrate the various kinds of reference materials and in verifying facts of publication.

I should like to express my appreciation to my family and to my friends and professional colleagues who cordially endorsed this endeavor; to my students whose favorable response to this approach to the subject of books and libraries encouraged me to put it into writing; and especially to my husband whose critical assistance and unfailing interest and encouragement were indispensable.

Jean Key Gates

INTRODUCTION

THE college library contributes to the program of the college by providing the books and materials which are required in the various phases of that program. The more diversified the college program, the greater the quantity and variety of library materials.

When a student enters college he finds a library which was planned and developed for work and study. He soon learns that the library is to become a part of his way of life. How much a part of his college experience it will become and how effectively it will contribute to his college years and to the years after college will depend upon his competence in using it.

Competence in the use of the library is a combination of attitudes, knowledge, and skills. It is dependent upon an awareness of the importance of books and libraries in our cultural heritage and in our daily life, a desire to use them, a knowledge of the kinds of materials which the library provides, and the development of skill in locating, selecting, using, describing, and evaluating these materials.

With the ever-increasing number, variety, and complexity of library materials and the emphasis upon teaching methods which place greater responsibility for learning upon the student himself, it becomes imperative that the college student begin in his freshman year to achieve a measure of competence in the use of the library. This competence should increase each year of his college career.

Some of the basic attitudes, knowledge, and skills which it is desirable for the student to achieve are:

1 An acquaintance with the history and development of books and libraries, an appreciation of their importance in our history and in our daily life, and a desire to use them

2 An understanding of the purpose of the college library, the kinds of materials it includes, and their physical arrangement and organization

3 A general idea of classification systems as an aid in the use of libraries

4 A knowledge of the purpose of the card catalog, the meaning for the student of each item of information on the catalog card, and the ways in which he can use this information

5 An ability to search for material beyond the catalog

6 A familiarity with the major reference books, both general and specialized: what they are and how to use them

7 Experience in the use of printed bibliographies

8 Experience in taking notes, compiling bibliographies, and making footnotes for term papers and research papers

9 Ability to decide upon the kinds of books and materials which are needed to answer a given question or to develop a given subject

10 An understanding of the importance of using a variety of sources

In general, each chapter includes (1) a definition of terms, (2) a brief statement of historical development, (3) discussion, and (4) appropriate examples.

Reference books are discussed as general or subject (specialized), according to kinds: dictionaries, indexes, handbooks, and others. Emphasis is placed on what they are, the purposes they serve, and the kinds of questions they are designed to answer, rather than on a mere listing of titles.

Since the student learns by doing, rather than by being told, it is necessary that all phases of his instruction be accompanied by learning experiences, with each experience built upon the preceding ones but introducing new materials. Suggested learning experiences are provided in the Instructor's Manual.

Technical library terminology is used only when it seems to be essential. The language is, with few exceptions, that of the student and the layman.

TABLE OF CONTENTS

Guide to the Use of Books and Libraries

✽ PART ONE ✽

THE LIBRARY

✄ CHAPTER ONE ✄

A BRIEF HISTORY OF BOOKS
AND LIBRARIES

Ancient peoples come upon the stage of history, not all together, but in a certain order, and by their proper entrances; each with a character and make-up congruous with the part they will play.[1]

THE story of these peoples—the order of their appearance, their accomplishments, their means of communication, and their relationships with each other—has been reconstructed in two ways: (1) from archaeological findings, which include tools, other products of their workmanship, and carvings and paintings on rock and stone; and (2) from written documents which record their achievements and their way of life.

The archaeological evidence belongs to the period of prehistory; the written records belong to the period of traditional history.

Written records depend upon the existence of a system of writing,

[1] *The Cambridge Ancient History* (2d ed.; New York: Cambridge University Press, 1924), I, 2.

a substance upon which to write, an instrument for writing, and a place to keep the finished products. The story of books and libraries from earliest times to the present is primarily the story of these systems of writing, the forms of the written documents, and the methods of preserving them and of making them accessible for use.

PRIMITIVE MEANS OF COMMUNICATION

Before prehistoric man learned that spoken words could be represented by visual symbols, his first means of communication may have been by gestures. To commemorate notable events or to establish landmarks he erected heaps of stones or boulders, called cairns. Knotted cords or beads served him as memory aids, and scratches on bronze or wood were messages he left for those who followed him.

Elders of the community memorized all that they considered was worth remembering, and they passed it on by word of mouth to succeeding generations. Collections of prayers, rituals, stories, and medical knowledge and the records of kings and priests were transmitted orally.

In time, men began to communicate with each other by means of crude pictures carved on rocks and stone. These carvings were of three kinds: (1) pictographic, representing an object; (2) ideographic, representing the idea suggested by the object; and (3) phonographic, representing the sound of the object or idea. Some of these ancient inscriptions can be interpreted. Crude picture writing was done on other materials which were at hand: vegetable fiber, cloth, wood, bark, animal skin, clay, and metal. However, only the writings on clay, metal, and stone have survived.

Most historians agree that all our systems of writing came from these crude carvings and picture writings.

WRITING, BOOKS, AND LIBRARIES

Antiquity: the Sumerians, Babylonians, and Assyrians From ca. 3600 to 2357 B.C. the Sumerian civilization flourished in the Tigris-Euphrates Valley, reaching its flower in the golden age of Ur, 2474 to

2398 B.C. As early as 3100 B.C., Sumerian historians began to record their current history and to reconstruct the story of their past.

The system of writing of the Sumerians, perhaps their greatest contribution to mankind, is the oldest system known. The word "cuneiform," which describes their style of writing, is from *cuneus*, the Latin word for wedge. The materials used were soft clay and a wedge-shaped stylus of metal, ivory, or wood. These are the earliest known writing materials which were used as we now use paper and pencil.

Writing was done by scribes who had been trained in professional schools to copy and memorize lists of words and names, to compose poetry, and to master mathematical problems. When the scribe had finished his writing, the clay was baked until it was hard as stone. These pieces of baked clay, small enough to be held in the hand of the scribe, are called tablets and were the first books.

To the Sumerians, writing was first of all a tool of trade and commerce. In addition, it was an instrument for recording religious works: prayers, ritual procedure, sacred legends, and magic formulas. On these clay tablets are also preserved the records of the first schools, the first social reforms, the first tax levies, and the first political, social, and philosophical thinking. It was several hundred years before the Sumerians produced literature, but among the tons of tablets and cylinders removed from the ruins of Sumeria's ancient cities are some containing literary works almost 1,000 years older than the *Iliad*. They constitute man's oldest known literature.

By 2700 B.C., the Sumerians had established private and religious, as well as government, libraries. Among these libraries was one at Tello which had a collection of over 30,000 tablets.

Sumeria declined in power after the sack of Ur by the Elamites ca. 2357 B.C., but her culture passed to Babylonia in Lower Mesopotamia, a civilization which lasted until 689 B.C. and which gave to mankind Hammurabi and his notable code of laws.

The Babylonians wrote on wet clay with a wedge-shaped stylus, as did the Sumerians. At first they used the Sumerian characters, but in time they changed and developed these characters to the extent that dictionaries which gave Sumerian words with their Babylonian equivalents became a necessity. Both Sumerian and Babylonian characters represented syllables rather than letters.

To the Babylonians, writing was primarily a device to be used in business transactions and in recording noteworthy events; thus their books were devoted to government, law, history, and religion. It is believed that there were many libraries in the temples and palaces of Babylonia. None of these survives, but the tablets of one of the most important ones, the library of Borsippa, were copied in their entirety by the scribes of Assurbanipal, King of Assyria, who preserved them in his library at Nineveh. These duplicates of the tablets from Borsippa are the chief sources of our knowledge of Babylonian life.

The Kingdom of Assyria, which also inherited its language and method of writing from Sumeria but modified the written characters until they resembled those of the Babylonians, existed at the same time as Babylonia. If it can be said that Sumeria's contribution to civilization was writing and that Babylonia's was law, then Assyria's gift to posterity was libraries.

The most important library in Assyria was established at Nineveh by Assurbanipal, who died about 626 B.C. Tens of thousands of clay tablets were brought to this great royal library by the king's scribes, who traveled throughout Babylonia and Assyria to copy and translate the writings they found. The catalog of the Nineveh Library was a listing of the contents of each cubicle or alcove, painted or carved on the entrance, where the clay tablets were arranged according to subject or type. Each tablet had an identification tag.

Among the most famous surviving specimens of cuneiform writing are the Code of Hammurabi,[2] now in the Louvre Museum in Paris, and the Gilgamesh Epic, part of which is the Babylonian story of the Flood. The key to this system of writing is the Behistun Inscription, which is located on the side of a mountain in Iran (Persia). Written in three languages (Persian, Babylonian, and Elamite), it was deciphered by Sir Henry Rawlinson when he was consul at Baghdad in 1844.

Antiquity: the Egyptians   The civilization of ancient Egypt flourished simultaneously with the Sumerian, Babylonian, and Assyrian civ-

---

[2] The Code of Hammurabi was not written on clay but was carved on a diorite cylinder. Diorite is a granular, crystalline, igneous rock.

ilizations. The earliest known writings of the Egyptians, who believed that the mere writing of a word would bring about the thought it expressed, date from ca. 3000 B.C.

The writing material was the papyrus sheet, and the instrument for writing was a brushlike pen made by fraying the edges of a reed. To make a papyrus sheet, the marrow of papyrus stalks was cut into thin strips and laid flat, side by side, one layer crossways over the other. The two layers were treated with a gum solution, pressed, pounded, and smoothed until the surface was suitable for writing, and then sized[3] to resist the ink.

The papyrus plant, a tall reedlike plant, grew in thick tufts in the marshy land along the Nile and was used by the Egyptians for purposes other than the making of writing material: the roots were dried and used for fuel; the fibers were made into rope; the stalks were used for thatching and for making light rafts; and in times of famine, the young shoots were used as food.

Papyrus was far from satisfactory as a writing material, for there was contant danger of punching through it in the process of writing. Also, it was susceptible to damage from water and dampness, and when it was dry, it was very fragile and brittle. In spite of these limitations, papyrus was the accepted writing material throughout the ancient Mediterranean world and is known to have been used as late as A.D. 1022.

The form of the book in ancient Egypt was the roll, usually a little more than 12 inches high and about 20 feet long, made from papyrus sheets pasted end to end. The style of writing was hieroglyphic, a word derived from the Greek *hieros,* meaning sacred, and *glyphein,* meaning to carve. Hieroglyphic writing, as old as the earliest Egyptian dynasty, was used as late as A.D. 394.

The Egyptians developed an alphabet of twenty-four consonants, but they did not adopt a completely alphabetic style of writing. They mixed pictographs, ideographs, and syllabic signs with their letters and developed a sketchy kind of writing for manuscripts, but the sacred carvings on their monuments were hieroglyphic.

Egyptian scribes were trained in the temple schools to learn to draw at least 700 different characters (hieroglyphs). Each scribe carried a writing

[3] Sizing was a process for filling the pores of the surface.

outfit containing a reed brush-pen, a little jar of water, and a palette with two depressions in which he could mix his inks.

Writing was done in columns without spaces between words, without punctuation marks, and usually without titles; the text began at the extreme right and continued right to left, and Egyptian rolls included religious, moral, and political subjects. The Prisse Papyrus in the Bibliothèque Nationale in Paris—the oldest Egyptian book known—is believed to have been written before the end of the third millennium (2880) B.C.; it contains the proverbial sayings of Ptahhotep. The longest Egyptian manuscript in existence, more than 130 feet long, is the Harris Papyrus, a chronicle of the reign of Rameses II.

The key to hieroglyphic writing is the Rosetta Stone, which was discovered near the mouth of the Nile in 1799 by a young officer of Napoleon's expeditionary force in Egypt. This flat slab of slate, bearing an inscription in three styles of writing—hieroglyphic, demotic (popular), and Greek—gave to Jean François Champollion, the French Egyptologist, the clue needed to decipher the Egyptian hieroglyphics. It is now preserved in the British Museum in London.

Little is known about Egyptian libraries. There may have been private and temple libraries as well as government archives. Records indicate that a library existed at Gizeh in the 2500s B.C., and it is known that Rameses II founded one at Thebes about 1250 B.C. Rolls were kept in clay jars or in metal cylinders with an identifying key word on the outside or on the end, or they were stacked on shelves.

Antiquity: Other Semitic Peoples   In addition to the Babylonians and the Assyrians, other Semitic peoples inhabited that part of the Near East known as the "Fertile Crescent."[4] Among them were the Phoenicians, the Aramaens, and the Hebrews.

Phoenicia was the name given in ancient times to a narrow strip of land about 100 miles long and 10 miles wide between Syria and the sea. The Phoenicians, whose ancestors may have come from Babylonia, belonged to the Canaanite branch of the Semites and called themselves Canaanites and their land Canaan. Although they claimed that their oldest cities were founded by the gods themselves and were 30,000 years

---

[4] The region bounded by the Taurus and the mountains of Armenia and Iran, the Persian Gulf, the Indian Ocean and the Red Sea, Egypt and the Mediterranean (*Cambridge Ancient History.* I, 182).

old, the establishment of Tyre has been placed at ca. 2756 B.C.[5] Among the chief cities of the Phoenicians were Tyre, Sidon, and Byblos.

Necessity, born of geographical location, made the Phoenicians a seafaring people, the busiest traders of the ancient world, and, after ca. 1200 B.C., masters of the Mediterranean.

> When your wares came from the seas,
>   you [Tyre] satisfied many peoples;
> with your abundant wealth and merchandise
>   you enriched the kings of the earth.[6]

An important item in the wares of the Phoenicians was papyrus, which they imported from Egypt and exported to all of the countries along the Mediterranean. It is believed that, wherever the Phoenicians took papyrus, they also took the Egyptian alphabet. History gives them major credit for spreading the knowledge and use of the alphabetic characters which had been developed in Egypt, Crete, and Syria and which form the basis of Greek and of all European writing.

The Phoenicians were not a literary people; writing and books were to them merely means of keeping their numerous commercial accounts. Their early writing bore a close resemblance to Hebrew, but they changed it into a cursive, flowing style and replaced the cumbersome clay tablets with papyrus sheets.

The Aramaens, whose first writing was in the cuneiform style of Mesopotamia, learned an alphabetic script either from the Egyptians or from the Phoenicians. Used first for commerce, this alphabetic writing of the Aramaens became a literary tool and the language of the Near East. It was the language of Christ and is the alphabet of the Arabs today.

The Hebrews lived in Palestine, a small country between Mesopotamia and Egypt, and their history is said to have begun ca. 2200 B.C. when Abraham left Ur in Chaldea to settle in the land of Canaan. Hebrew writing dates from Moses and the Tables of Law, but their most ancient pieces of written literature, inscriptions in the old Canaanite script, date only from ca. 1200 B.C. Their most brilliant literary period was that which produced the works of the Old Testament.

---

[5] Based on the statement made by Herodotus in book II, paragraph 44, that he was told that Tyre was founded 2,300 years before his visit.

[6] Ezek. 27:33. Revised Standard Version.

Writing materials were papyrus, leather, and parchment, together with reed brush or quill, and their book forms were the roll and the tablet. Their libraries were connected to the temple. The language of the Hebrews, with an alphabet of twenty-two consonants similar to those of the Phoenicians, was the purest and most complete of the Semitic family of languages.

Antiquity: the Chinese   The art of writing was known in China as early as the third millennium B.C. Materials on which the Chinese wrote included bone, tortoise shell, bamboo stalks, wooden tablets, silk, and linen, and their writing instruments were the stylus, the quill, and the brush-pen, depending upon the particular writing material used. The style of writing involved the use of characters, mainly ideographic, and book forms were the tablet and the roll. Little is known about their libraries.

Antiquity: the Greeks   The Greeks called their country Hellas and themselves Hellēnes, and during the 1,200-year period of Greek civilization, ending in 146 B.C. with the Roman conquest, they dominated the world from Sicily to the Black Sea and from the Balkans to North Africa.

Although written records date from only about 776 B.C., the epic poems of Homer (perhaps about the ninth century B.C.) and Hesiod (perhaps about the eighth century B.C.), handed down by word of mouth, picture the life of the ancient Greeks—their wars, their seafaring adventures, and their daily life. Of the seventh and sixth centuries B.C., only fragments of literature remain, but these fragments show the beginnings of new forms of poetry, notably the elegy and the choral lyric, and the birth of philosophy and scientific research. The fables of Aesop date from this period.

The fifth century brought the golden age of Greek civilization, a period characterized by the highest form of literary creativity: the tragedies of Sophocles, Aeschylus, and Euripides; the lyric poetry of Pindar; the histories of Thucydides and Herodotus; the comedies of Aristophanes; and the philosophy of Socrates. This period of high literary and intellectual creativity, also referred to as the Classical Age, extended through the fourth and into the third centuries B.C., finding expression in the works of Plato and Aristotle, as well as in drama, poetry, oration, and music.

The Hellenistic period, dating from the death of Alexander in 323

B.C. to the Roman conquest, saw a continuation of the literary activities of the preceding century and a new emphasis on scientific knowledge (in the works of Euclid and Archimedes), on art, and on rhetoric. Through commerce, conquest, and colonization, Greek culture and civilization spread throughout the Mediterranean and Asiatic world, and when Rome conquered Greece in 146 B.C., Rome herself was already strongly influenced by the civilization of Greece. Through Rome, Greek thought, art, and culture formed the foundation of the civilization of Western Europe, influencing its culture and ethics, its law and government, its art and architecture, its literature and science, and even its athletic games.

There are no actual specimens of books from the first 600 years of Greek civilization. There were probably schools, books, and a limited reading public in Athens by the sixth century. The development of civilization in the fifth century created a need for the extension of education, and while there seems to have been little emphasis on book production as such, there must have been a plentiful supply of books accessible to those who wanted to read them. During the Hellenistic period, books were produced on a large scale under the patronage of the Hellenistic monarchs.

In ancient Greece the materials used to receive writing were leaves or bark of trees, stone or bronze for inscriptions, and wax-coated wooden tablets for messages or notes. From the sixth century B.C., papyrus, which the Phoenicians brought from Egypt, was the usual writing material. In Hellenistic Greece, parchment and vellum came into use.

Parchment was the skin of animals, principally that of the sheep or the calf, prepared for writing. The skin was not tanned but was washed carefully and then covered with lime to loosen the hair; after the hair was removed, each skin was stretched on a frame, scraped, dusted with sifted chalk, and polished with pumice. The use of parchment made necessary the development of a new kind of writing instrument, the broadpointed pen made from a reed or a quill. The appearance of the writing produced by this pen was quite different from the brushlike strokes on papyrus. Parchment proved to be a better medium for writing than papyrus because it was smooth on both sides and was less likely to tear. Papyrus competed with it for three centuries, however, and only in the fourth century A.D. did parchment become dominant.

Vellum, which is made from the skin of calves, is heavier than parchment and more expensive. It is probably the most beautiful and the most lasting material ever used for books.

The forms of Greek books were the roll, the wax tablet, and the codex, in which the papyrus or parchment leaves of the manuscript were fastened together as in a modern book. The subject matter of Greek books included literature, history, science, mathematics, philosophy, religion, politics, and all of the other facets of their civilization and culture.

Early Greek writing resembled that of the Phoenicians, who had brought them the alphabet, but gradually the Greeks changed the form of the letters, added vowels, changed some consonants to vowels, developed lower-case letters, and began writing from left to right. The first books did not have spaces between words or punctuation marks of any kind. Change from one topic to another was indicated by a horizontal dividing stroke called the *paragraphos,* and if the roll had a title, it was located at the end. Before the conquest of Greece by the Romans, Greek grammarians had introduced some forms of punctuation.

There are evidences of private libraries in the fifth century B.C. The important library of Euripides was followed by other private libraries, notably that of Aristotle. In Hellenistic Greece there were private, governmental, and royal libraries, but the most important ones were in the outposts of the empire. The greatest library of all was at Alexandria in Egypt, founded during the reign of Ptolemy I (323–283 B.C.), who gave to Demetrius the task and honor of administering it. It is reported to have grown under his direction to 200,000 rolls within five years. It is said that foreigners were required, upon entering the Alexandria harbor, to surrender any books in their possession, later receiving copies in exchange for the originals. At the time of the Roman conquest the Alexandrian Library contained 700,000 rolls, including manuscripts from all parts of the known world, written in Egyptian, Hebrew, Latin, and other languages. As the political importance of Alexandria declined, the library suffered; many volumes were burned by the Romans, and it was completely destroyed when the Moslems conquered Egypt.[7]

Second in importance to the library at Alexandria was the one at Pergamum, founded by Eumenes II (197–159 B.C.). According to Plu-

[7] Fragments of Greek literary works have been found in great quantities in the papyri discovered by archaeologists in Egypt.

tarch, Calvisius, a friend of Caesar, charged that Antony gave to Cleopatra the entire library of Pergamum, which contained 200,000 distinct volumes.[8] Pergamum became outstanding for the patronage of arts and letters, and book production was so intense that an embargo was placed by the Egyptians on the exportation of papyrus, with the hope of discouraging the copying of books. This act led to the increased production of parchment for use as a writing material.

Antiquity: the Romans   Through commerce with Greece, Rome (which was founded in 753 B.C.) had early adopted the Greek alphabet, and Greek culture became important in Rome following the first Punic War (264–241 B.C.). By the time of the Roman conquest of Greece, the Romans were under the influence of the Greeks to the extent that they read and studied their literature, philosophy, and science, sent their sons to Athens to be educated, and at times spoke Greek. Thus, having adopted the Greek tradition in books, the Romans continued it. Latin literature began in the second century B.C.

The materials which the Romans used for writing were papyrus, parchment, vellum, wood tablets coated with wax, the stylus, the split-point reed, and the split-feather quill. Incidentally, our word "pen" comes from the Latin word for feather.

The Romans developed a style of handwriting unlike the ordinary cursive writing for use in literary works. Much like the Greek, it consisted largely of capital letters. By the end of the fourth century A.D., another style called uncial script, which involved the use of large, somewhat rounded letters, was the standard book script and continued as such until the end of the eighth century.

The forms of the book in ancient Rome were the roll, the wax tablet, the diptych (two boards hinged together at one side with waxed surfaces on the inside for writing), and the codex.

Since the roll was relatively inconvenient to write upon and to read, it was superseded inevitably by the more usable form, the codex, which was used to some extent by the Greeks and which is known to have been in use among the Christians in the second century A.D. From that time the codex generally was used for Christian works, even though the papyrus roll was continued in use for pagan works.

---

[8] *Plutarch's Lives of Illustrious Men*, corrected from the Greek and revised by A. H. Clough (Boston: Little, Brown & Company, 1930), p. 674.

Roman books included all known fields of knowledge: law, science, mathematics, philosophy, politics, and religious and secular literature. The earliest known fragment of a manuscript book is the Papyrus Rylands, a tiny piece of a papyrus leaf of the Gospel according to St. John, dated (from the style of writing) in the first half of the second century A.D. The Codex Vaticanus of the fourth century A.D. is the oldest extant manuscript of antiquity.

Roman generals brought back entire libraries from the campaigns in Greece, and these libraries, considered spoils of war, became their private collections. In fact, collecting books and building libraries became a fad among the wealthy, even those who could not read. A sizable book collection was considered by every prominent Roman to be an essential part of his house.

Cicero (106–43 B.C.) had a private library in each of his villas. Sulla captured Athens in 86 B.C. and with it the library of Aristotle. The most important library of this period was that of Lucullus (ca. 114–57 B.C.). Plutarch refers to it in this manner:

> His furnishing a library . . . deserves praise and record, for he collected very many choice manuscripts; and the use they were put to was even more magnificent than the purchase, the library being always open, and the walks and reading-rooms about it free to all Greeks.[9]

Julius Caesar drew up plans for public libraries, but since his plans were not carried out until the reign of Augustus, credit for establishing the first public library in Rome, between 39 and 27 B.C., is given to Asinius Pollio. By the middle of the fourth century A.D. there were at least twenty-eight public libraries in Rome, and they were used by any person, slave or free, who could read.

The Ulpian Library in the Forum of Trajan was probably typical of Roman libraries. Greek works were kept on one side of the library, and Latin works were placed on the other side; they were arranged according to subject on shelves or in bins. Except in rare cases, books had to be used in the reading rooms.

The era of Roman libraries lasted 500 years. They were destroyed in the barbarian invasions, and the information which we have about

[9] *Ibid.*, p. 367.

them came from the ruined cities of Pompeii and Herculaneum, which were destroyed by Vesuvius in A.D. 79. In the famous library found in the ruins of Herculaneum were hundreds of charred papyrus rolls in the ruins of book cases which stood around the room. In the center of the room was a table. It is believed that this room was typical of Roman libraries of that time.

The Middle Ages: Monasteries With the disintegration of the Roman Empire came the decline of classical culture. During the Dark Ages (ca. 400–900 A.D.), all libraries, including Christian collections, suffered at the hands of barbarians. Some secular literature was transferred to Constantinople where it was kept in the libraries and monasteries of the Moslem Empire, and many Christian writings were collected and preserved in the monasteries of Christian monks.

The institution of monasticism was of major importance in the preservation and development of literature during the Middle Ages. In the sixth century Cassiodorus established the Vivarium Monastery in southern Italy with a scriptorium (writing room) where manuscripts were copied by the monks. St. Columban founded the monasteries of Luxeuil in France and Bobbio in northern Italy in the sixth and seventh centuries, respectively. St. Boniface established monasteries in Germany in the eighth century and contributed to the literary development of his native England by seeking numerous copies of English works for his monastery libraries, notably the one at Fulda.

Manuscripts were copied and recopied by the monks in countless scriptoria throughout England, Ireland, Europe, and the Moslem Empire. These manuscripts tell us much of what we know of the ancient world. In these institutions were preserved the books of our Bible, the epics of Homer, the poetry of Virgil, the Greek dramas, and the scientific, legal, and philosophical works of the great minds of antiquity.

Alcuin of York, following in the tradition of Cassiodorus, St. Columban, and St. Boniface and with the patronage of Charlemagne, was able to build a great library at his abbey in Tours, bringing books from all over the known world to be copied by the monks. Alcuin was also influential in introducing a system of education and in founding schools. This interest in learning eventually spread throughout Europe.

The chief materials used by the monks for writing were plain or dyed parchment or vellum, quill pens, and many kinds of colored inks.

The writing style of the monks developed into national styles at various monasteries. The forms of the book were the roll and the codex.

Copying books by hand was tedious and painful. *Scriptores,* or writers, sat or stood at sloping desks and copied for hours. A scribe might complete three to five large leaves in a day; at that rate, it took about a year to copy the Bible. When a monk had finished his copying, the manuscript was given to another monk for correction, and to still another monk for illumination—a decoration of ornamental letters, scrolls, and miniatures—if this was required.

The style of copying was determined by the nature of the book. For example, the Scriptures, because of their importance and volume, had a special style. The earliest books were plain, but eventually the beginning letters were illuminated; then the margins were decorated with elaborate designs; the opening pages were given an ornamental border; and miniatures—small paintings in color—were introduced. The principal colors were red, blue, and gold, and sometimes purple, yellow, and green. An entire manuscript might be lettered in gold and silver on parchment which was dyed purple. One of the most famous examples of beautiful manuscript books, and of Irish illuminated art, is the *Book of Kells,* an illuminated manuscript of the four Gospels dating from the eighth century.

The story of another beautiful manuscript book, copied more than 700 years after the *Book of Kells,* illustrates dramatically the art, skill, and dedication of the medieval scribe.[10]

> About the middle of the fifteenth century, a wealthy businessman went to the master scribe at a copyist's guild or scriptorium in Germany and left an order to have the Bible copied. No expense was to be spared; material and workmanship were to be the finest. It was to be richly and handsomely ornamented, not by the usual staff of illuminators, but by the best artists that could be found. As to size, it must be comparable to the tremendous Bibles the businessman had seen in his travels in Austria and England.

[10] Adapted from Dorothy Miner, *The Giant Bible of Mainz: 500th Anniversary* (Washington: The Library of Congress, 1952), pp. 3–5. This famous work was presented to the Library of Congress by Mr. Lessing J. Rosenwald in 1952. It is usually displayed in the Library of Congress in conjunction with another fine, large Bible, the Gutenberg Bible, which was produced about the same time, not by hand but printed with movable types.

The shops of the local parchment makers were searched for the largest sheets of vellum of the finest quality, unblemished, soft and supple, so that the great pages could be turned without noisy crackling, and of a brilliant whiteness with a velvety surface that would hold ink and illuminator's colors firmly. The text was to be in two columns for easy reading, but the margins were to be very wide to allow for elaborate illumination.

Ordinarily the work would have been assigned to several scribes, but for this special task the master scribe would do all the writing. On April 4, 1452, the scribe began his work. He worked for many months without hurry. When he became tired, he turned to other tasks so that the great book would never show a faltering hand. At the end of each book of the Bible, he noted the date on which he reached that point. On July 9, 1453, fifteen months after he began, the master scribe finished his task, and thus was produced "The Giant Bible of Mainz."

Early monastic libraries were small. Manuscripts were expensive: a large Bible was bought for 10 talents (about $10,000), and a missal was exchanged for a vineyard. A monastery library would have many copies of the Bible, the service books of the church, lives of the saints, early Christian writings, law, poetry, and some classical works.

Books were kept in chests or cupboards, or they were brought out and chained to desks for safety. Most of the reading was done standing up. In general, books were arranged by subject or kind—religious or secular, Greek or Latin. At first, catalogs were rough check lists. Later, a fuller and more precise description of the book and its contents was given in the listing.

The Middle Ages: Universities From the fall of Rome to the twelfth century, education was in the hands of the monastery, and instruction was chiefly theological. Some instruction was given to sons of noblemen and, in some cases, to promising children of the poor. In trading centers there were schools to train clerks. In the École Palatine, the academy founded by Charlemagne ca. 782, women as well as men were educated.

By the middle of the twelfth century, men were going to school to study Latin grammar and other basic subjects. The rise of cathedral schools, the study of Latin grammar, the appearance of writing in the

vernacular (the language of the masses), and the increasingly favorable
social and economic conditions gave rise to the universities.

The university of this period was a group of teachers organized as
a kind of guild and empowered by either religious or civil government to
grant degrees. The outstanding universities of the Middle Ages were
the universities of Bologna, Paris, Prague, Heidelberg, Oxford, and Cambridge.

Book dealers (*stationarii*) and their scribes were an important part
of every medieval university. They were appointed or controlled by the
university to guarantee the authenticity of texts. They kept in stock correct editions of books used for instruction and rented them to the students. Dealers in parchment and vellum were licensed by the university.
Since the universities constituted both the chief supply of books and the
chief demand for them, they became the main centers of the book trade
and of the publishing (copying) business. Book forms were the roll and
the codex.

There was little need for libraries as long as the students could rent
the texts they needed. However, as the number of students increased, the
universities were forced to establish libraries. In time, books were given
by individuals to the universities for the use of students.

Each college within a university had its own library. Arrangement
and organization were similar to those of the larger monastery libraries
except that books were divided according to the subject taught. They
were arranged according to size or accession, sometimes on shelves rather
than in chests. The more important books were still chained to the desks,
but in some libraries, the chains were lengthened so that the student
could take his book to a nearby table and sit down while he studied.

The Middle Ages: Printing with Movable Types   Not until the
fourteenth and fifteenth centuries did the middle classes attain the social,
intellectual, and economic level which made it possible for them to own
books. Three developments in these centuries helped to make books accessible to the middle class: (1) books were written in the national language, (2) the use of paper for writing made books more plentiful and
much less expensive, and (3) the invention of printing with movable
types increased greatly the supply of books of all kinds.

The success of printing depended upon a cheap substance on which
to print, an ink which would adhere to type, a press which could apply

heavy pressure over a large frame, and a general knowledge of metal technology.

By the second quarter of the fifteenth century, these needs had been met. Paper was a cheap and plentiful material on which to print. Discovered in China in the second century but used little by the Chinese, paper had traveled west along the trade routes. It was brought to Persia in the eighth century; it was displacing papyrus in Egypt in the ninth century; the Moslems used it in Spain in the eleventh and twelfth centuries; it was manufactured in southern Italy in 1270; and by the end of the fourteenth century, it was manufactured in France and Germany. The material used in making paper was linen rags. These rags were softened to a pulp and molded into sheets on a wooden frame. The sheets were drained, pressed and pressed again, hung to dry completely, and then sized to make them impervious to ink.

A suitable ink was developed by adapting the oil paints which the artists of the time were using.

The screw presses which were used for pressing olives and grapes and in binding manuscript books were used to apply pressure over a large frame.

The general knowledge of metal technology, which was essential to the success of printing, was borrowed from the goldsmiths and silversmiths. Carving of wood blocks for wood-block printing and engraving on metal by goldsmiths and silversmiths had reached a high degree of perfection. This knowledge was easily transferred to the process of making metal types.

Perhaps no event in the cultural history of mankind exceeds in importance the invention of printing with movable types.[11] Learning, which was formerly confined to monasteries or available only to the student,

11 The Babylonians and the Egyptians had used metal or wooden seals to print on soft clay or on wax; the Romans printed symbols on coins and stamped official documents with a carved seal; as early as the fifth and sixth centuries, the Chinese used carved seals to print short mottoes and charms. The full-page woodcut, printed from a wooden block on which the text and illustrations had been carved, was the next step in printing. By the ninth century, the Chinese produced a complete book printed in this manner. This kind of book was called a block book. The *Diamond Sutra*, a block book printed in A.D. 868, has survived. By the tenth century, printing in this manner was common in China. In Europe there were woodcut prints by the fourteenth century.

particularly the wealthy student, was now within reach of any person who wished to pursue it.

Movable word types made of clay originated in China but were used very little. It is to John Gutenberg, born in Mainz, Germany, about 1400, that credit is given for the development of printing with movable types. His creative genius combined the available materials and supplied the remaining essentials which made possible the printing of the famous 42-line Bible between 1450 and 1456. This was the first book printed with movable types.

The printed book was new only with regard to the way it was made; it was not new in appearance. The types were similar to manuscript writing. Space was left for illumination and rubrication, which were done by hand. The first illustrations were woodcuts. This similarity to the handwritten book continued for more than a hundred years.

When all paper was made by hand, the sheets were of about the same size. The number of times the sheet was folded to make the pages of a book indicated the size of the book. If a full sheet was folded to make two leaves of four pages, it was said to be in folio; four leaves of eight pages, quarto; eight leaves of sixteen pages, octavo; and so forth.

The first printed works are called incunabula (from the Latin word *incunabulum* meaning cradle), indicating that printing was in its infancy. The subject matter of early printed books included the Bible and other religious works, textbooks, histories, travel books, and literature of all kinds.

During the last quarter of the fifteenth century, printing spread to all major cities of Europe. More than 20,000 different works and editions of this period survive. The sixteenth century is notable for the rise of a large number of printing families, each with its own specialty. The House of Estienne, for example, printed Greek and Latin classics. The printer Geoffroy Tory was responsible for introducing the accent, the apostrophe, and the cedilla into the French language, and Aldus Manutius developed a system of punctuation marks. By 1700 the printed book had reached its present form, with a title page, illustrations, a table of contents, and even a kind of index.

The invention of printing, a product of the intellectual curiosity and freedom which characterized the Renaissance, provided an unparalleled and effective impetus to the rebirth of learning. Precious manuscripts of the past, formerly copied one at a time by hand, could be reproduced in multiple copies and passed on to those who so eagerly sought them. The printing press also encouraged, by making written works quickly available, the production of new literature, and in this way it helped to create the "professional man of letters." The printing press and the increased dissemination of printed materials contributed importantly to the success of the Reformation, and the stimulus which it gave to map making hastened the era of discovery and exploration. With the invention of printing came the beginning of the modern era.

The Modern Era: 1500–1900   Books after 1500 varied widely both in format and in content. There were many large volumes, many very small ones. Bookbindings ranged from ornate, bejewelled, gold-tooled leather to plain vellum and, eventually, paper. Printing types ceased to be copies of manuscript writing and assumed an identity all their own. In the sixteenth and seventeenth centuries periodicals were published; in the late seventeenth century newspapers appeared. The first modern encyclopedia was published in Switzerland in 1630.

The contents of books during these centuries included religious and classical subjects, as well as science, superstition, travel, and romance.

The nineteenth century brought new mechanical developments, including stereotyping and the cylinder press. Some books were printed in colored ink; one book is known to have been printed in four colors: red, blue, orange, and violet. The nineteenth century saw much fine printing, especially in England. Wood came into use as a source for paper, books were bound with cloth, and copyright legislation was enacted.

The oldest book known to have been printed in Colonial America was the Bay Psalm Book, printed in 1640. The first printing press was established in Boston in 1675. Benjamin Franklin was Colonial America's most outstanding printer.

The almanac was the colonial printer's usual publication. Others were newspapers, broadsides, religious and political pamphlets, official government publications, religious books, classics, and books on the social sciences and literature. The first American magazine was published in 1741, several others were published before 1775, but none survived the Revolution.

The Constitution of the United States recognized the importance of the printer and of printing in Article I of the Bill of Rights, which guarantees freedom of the press.

In Europe, libraries flourished during the period from 1500 to 1900. Italy was outstanding for the number and quality of libraries in the sixteenth century. The Laurentian Library in Venice, the Ambrosian Library in Milan, and the Vatican Library in Rome were the most important.

In France, the Bibliothèque Nationale (which had its origins in the collections formed by the kings of France and may be said to date from Francis I, who assembled the royal collections at Fontainebleau) was moved to Paris by Charles IX (1560–1574) and was greatly expanded and enlarged by Louis XIV (1643–1715). As early as 1692, it was open to the public twice a week.

Germany had the finest libraries of the nineteenth century. State libraries and university libraries were outstanding for size, content, and organization. There were also circulating libraries with catalogs, popular reading rooms, and children's collections.

The Oxford and Cambridge libraries and the British Museum (the National Library) were the most important in England.

The Austrian Royal Library, the royal library at Brussels, and the university libraries at Ghent and Louvain were other important libraries founded between 1500 and 1900.

The first colleges in the American Colonies—Harvard (1638), William and Mary (1695), Yale (1700), and Princeton (1746)—began with, or were accompanied by, gifts of books. Although the Massachusetts General Court voted in 1636 to set aside 400 pounds for the establishment of a "schoole or colledge," Harvard was not opened until 1638 when John Harvard bequeathed to the new college one-half of his estate and his entire library of 320 volumes. Yale College began with forty books. Each of the eleven clergymen who met in 1700 for the purpose of forming a college brought a number of books which he gave "for the founding of a college in this colony" (Connecticut). Most of the volumes in the early college libraries were books on theology, but there were also copies of the classics and of philosophical and literary works. By 1725 Harvard had 3,000 books, thus having the largest college library in the colonies.

In the early college libraries there was no effort to make books available to students; rather, it seemed, books were protected from the students. This protective attitude continued throughout the nineteenth century, and as late as the 1850s, some college libraries were open only one hour every two weeks, others one hour twice a week, and a few one hour a day. In some libraries, attempts were made to classify books into three groups: memory, judgment, and imagination; or history, philosophy, and poetry. In others, books were arranged according to appearance, accession, or donor. The location symbol for books gave the physical location only and did not indicate the class to which the book belonged. Catalogs were printed lists, with little information about books.

Books were expensive and scarce, since most of them had to be brought from abroad. The important private libraries of the early colonial period were those of Elder Brewster of the Plymouth Colony (about 400 different works), John Winthrop (over 1,000 volumes), and Cotton and Increase Mather. In Virginia, books were owned even by the yeoman class.

The Library of Congress was established in 1800. Burned by the British in 1814, it was reestablished in 1815 with the purchase of Thomas Jefferson's library. The first tax-supported library in the United States was established in Peterborough, New Hampshire, in 1833. The Boston Public Library, founded in 1854, marked the beginning of the public library movement in America. The year 1876 was full of significance for libraries in the United States because during that year Melville Dewey published the first edition of his *Decimal Classification,* and the American Library Association was organized. In 1887 the first library school for the training of professional librarians was established at Columbia University with Melville Dewey as its head.

By 1890 the public library had become an established institution in America, and the organization and development of libraries was given added impetus after that time by the state library commissions, which were established to aid in founding libraries and in improving and extending their services.

The Modern Era: the Twentieth Century   In the twentieth century, all libraries have been characterized by enormous growth in size and in importance. This growth has been made possible by increased local interest, by a recognition of the importance of libraries in the educational, social, and cultural life of a democratic society, and by the munificent gifts of private philanthropy. The greatest individual benefactor of libraries was Andrew Carnegie, whose gifts totaled over forty million dollars. Other benefactors include the Rockefeller and Ford Foundations and individual philanthropists who have opened their collections of rare books to the public. Examples of rare-book libraries are the Pierpont Morgan Library in New York City and the Folger Shakespeare Library in Washington, D.C.

Each state has made legal provision for public library service, and the state library commission is authorized to aid in founding local, county, and multicounty libraries. The public library is now recognized as a valuable complement to the public school in educating for democratic living. In carrying out this function, it provides special services for children and young people; promotes educational, civic, and cultural programs; makes special materials available to the handicapped; supplements school library collections; and carries library materials to rural and isolated areas via the bookmobile.

Although school libraries were authorized by law in some states as early as 1835, it was not until the 1930s that they began to make a significant contribution to school programs. Since the 1940s school libraries have placed emphasis upon use as well as upon number of volumes. Elementary-school libraries have not progressed as rapidly as have secondary-school libraries, and in many areas elementary schools are still dependent upon the state library or a nearby public library for loans of books. However, new standards for elementary-school libraries, adopted by the American Library Association in 1960, should result in great advances in the number, as well as in the use, of libraries in the elementary school.

Special libraries in law, medicine, technology, music, and other subject areas, as well as libraries in special types of institutions, are new developments in the twentieth century.

The American college library has entered upon a period of growth, not only in terms of number of volumes, but even more significantly, in terms of its importance in the college academic program. In 1959–1960, according to the United States Office of Education, the libraries of the 2,011 institutions of higher education in the United States contained approximately 167 million volumes.

The college library of today is not a separate institution but is an integral part of the college; it exists only to help the college carry out its objectives. The method of teaching a subject rather than a textbook has necessitated wide and intensive use of the library. The college library seeks to provide and make easily accessible to the student the materials he needs for class assignments and for voluntary and recreational reading.

The book in the twentieth century is the printed book, ranging from fine leather-bound volumes to paperbacks; it is the microfilm and the microcard (microscopic photographs of books and newspapers which must be read with the aid of a reading machine); it is the periodical, the pamphlet, and the newspaper; and in the rare-book rooms of many twentieth-century libraries and museums, it is also the clay tablet, the papyrus or parchment roll, the illuminated manuscript, the vellum codex, and the incunabulum.

BIBLIOGRAPHY

General

Dahl, Svend. *History of the Book.* New York: Scarecrow Press, 1958.

The Encyclopaedia Britannica: A Dictionary of Arts, Sciences, Literature and General Information. 11th ed. London: Cambridge University Press, 1910–1911. 26 vols.

Hessel, Alfred. *History of Libraries.* 2d ed. Translated by Reuben Peiss. New York: Scarecrow Press, 1955.

Irwin, Keith Gordon. *The Romance of Writing from Egyptian Hieroglyphics to Modern Letters, Numbers, and Signs.* New York: The Viking Press, Inc., 1956.

Langer, William L. (ed.). *An Encyclopedia of World History, Ancient, Medieval, and Modern, Chronologically Arranged.* Boston: Houghton Mifflin Company, 1952.

Larousse, Pierre Athanase. *Grand Dictionnaire Universel du XIXe Siècle Français.* Paris: Larousse, 1865–1890. 17 vols.

"Libraries," *The Encyclopedia Americana,* 1958 ed., vol. XVII.

McMurtrie, Douglas C. *The Book: The Story of Printing & Bookmaking.* 3d ed. New York: Oxford University Press, 1943.

Antiquity

Barnett, Lincoln. "The Epic of Man," Part VI: "The Oldest Nation: Egypt," *Life*, XLI (October 1, 1956), 78–98.

Bury, J. B., Cook, S. A., and Adcock, F. E. (eds.). *The Cambridge Ancient History*. 2d ed. Vol. I: *Egypt and Babylonia to 1580 B.C.* New York: Cambridge University Press, 1924.

Durant, Will. *The Story of Civilization*. Vol. I: *Our Oriental Heritage*. New York: Simon and Schuster, Inc., 1942.

Finegan, Jack. *Light From the Ancient Past: The Archaeological Background of the Hebrew-Christian Religion*. 2d ed. Princeton: Princeton University Press, 1959.

Harvey, Sir Paul (ed.). *The Oxford Companion to Classical Literature*. 2d ed. New York: Oxford University Press, 1937.

Herodotus. *The History of Herodotus*. Translated by George Rawlinson. New York: Tudor Publishing Company, 1941.

Kenyon, Frederic George. *Books and Readers in Ancient Greece and Rome*. 2d ed. New York: Oxford University Press, 1951.

Kramer, Samuel Noah. *From the Tablets of Sumer*. Indian Hills, Colo.: Falcon's Wing Press, 1956.

———. "The Sumerians," *Scientific American*, XXVII (October, 1957), 70–87.

Lissner, Ivar. *The Living Past*. Translated from the German by J. Maxwell Brownjohn. New York: G. P. Putnam's Sons, 1957.

National Geographic Magazine. *Everyday Life in Ancient Times: Highlights of Western Civilization in Mesopotamia, Egypt, Greece, and Rome*. Washington, D.C.: National Geographic Magazine, 1958.

Plutarchus. *Plutarch's Lives of Illustrious Men*. The Translation Called Dryden's. Corrected from the Greek and revised by A. H. Clough. Boston: Little, Brown & Company, 1930.

The Middle Ages

Durant, Will. *The Story of Civilization*. Vol. IV: *The Age of Faith*. New York: Simon and Schuster, Inc., 1942.

Harvey, Sir Paul, and Heseltine, J. E. (eds.). *The Oxford Companion to French Literature*. New York: Oxford University Press, 1959.

Haskins, Charles Homer. *The Renaissance of the Twelfth Century*. Cambridge, Mass.: Harvard University Press, 1927.

Thompson, James Westfall. *The Medieval Library*. New York: Hafner Publishing Company, 1957.

Coulton, George G. "Universities." *A Cyclopedia of Education*. 1913 ed. Vol. V.

Colleges in the American Colonies

Morison, Samuel Eliot. *The Intellectual Life of Colonial New England*. 2d ed. New York: New York University Press, 1956.

Wright, Louis B. *The Cultural Life of the American Colonies, 1607–1763*. New York: Harper & Brothers, 1957.

CHAPTER TWO

THE COLLEGE LIBRARY

THE word "college," from the Latin word meaning a society, was used originally to refer to a group of persons who had common interests or functions, such as a body of clergy living in common in a monastery. With the rise of universities in the Middle Ages, the name college was given to a group of scholars incorporated for study or instruction in the higher branches of knowledge, a college being one of several schools of a university.

From this latter meaning, with some additions and alterations, comes the definition in use today. In general, the name college is given to an institution of higher learning not divided into separate schools and faculties, which offers a four-year curriculum leading to a degree in arts and sciences and which requires for admission graduation from an accredited secondary school or its equivalent.

Our word "library" comes from the Latin *liber*, meaning book, through the French *librairie*, which means bookseller's shop, and *libraire*, which means copyist. Medieval universities did not provide books for students but appointed and controlled the booksellers and copyists who rented or sold the texts which students needed for study and reference. Thus inherent in the word library is the idea of providing materials for use, and the college library today, like the bookseller's shop of the medieval university, provides the books and materials which students need for study and reference. The college library is a building or a series of rooms containing a collection of books and other materials which have been acquired and prepared for the use of students, faculty, and others.

FUNCTION AND ORGANIZATION OF THE COLLEGE LIBRARY

The primary function of the college library is to aid the college in carrying out its program. The nature of the college determines its objectives and program, and the library contributes to the realization of these objectives by acquiring and making available the books and other materials needed in the instructional program of the college.

In order to carry out its responsibility in the college program effectively, the library performs certain activities:

1 It selects books and materials. This selection is based upon study and evaluation of available materials and upon requests from the faculty and other members of the college community. It acquires these materials chiefly through purchases and gifts.

2 It prepares these materials for the use of students, faculty, and others who require them. This preparation includes:

  a Stamping, pasting, typing, and lettering.

  b Classifying materials according to the classification system in use by the library and assigning book numbers. (The classification number and the book number make the call number of a book.)

  c Cataloging these materials, that is, providing descriptive information about each one as to author, title, facts of publication, number of pages, illustrative material, and other information; assigning subject headings and making cross references; and maintaining the card catalog and other card files.

3 It circulates materials from the general collection and from the reserve collection. (Reserve books are those books in which class assignments have been made; they are kept together in one place.)

4 It gives reference service, answering questions, preparing bibliographies and reading lists, and borrowing and lending materials on interlibrary loan.

5 It gives instruction in the use of the library, in either formal classes or lectures and by aiding readers in the use of the card catalog, reference books, and other materials and facilities.

6 It administers the total library program, including the budget, the organization and supervision of the various library activities, the maintenance of the building and equipment, and the public relations activities.

In most libraries, these activities are divided into departments such as the acquisitions department, the cataloging department, the circulation department, and the reference department, all of which are under the administrative head of the library. These departments may be subdivided according to specific activities; they may be combined; and they may be given different names. Whatever the nature of the administrative organization of the library, varying as it does according to the size of the college, the size of the staff, and other factors, its aim is to serve the college instructional program efficiently.

KINDS OF MATERIALS PROVIDED BY THE COLLEGE LIBRARY

The quantity and diversity of library materials will vary according to the size, purpose, and program of the college, but in most college libraries materials will include:

1 Reference books of a general nature and reference books in the subject fields, with emphasis upon the subject areas included in the college instructional program. These reference books include dictionaries, encyclopedias, indexes, yearbooks, handbooks, atlases, gazetteers, bibliographies, and certain collected works like the *Cambridge Ancient History* and the *Cambridge History of American Literature*.

2 A collection of books containing:

a Books which relate to and supplement each curriculum offered, such as history, education, and foreign languages, including those books which cover the entire field and those which relate to the specific courses offered in that field

b Important general books not relating to a specific subject area, and important books in subject fields not included in the college curriculums

c Books for voluntary and recreational reading

3 Periodicals and newspapers—current issues, bound volumes, and in some libraries, those on microfilm and microcards.

4 Pamphlets and clippings.

5 Audio-visual materials, which include pictures, motion-picture films, slides, filmstrips, music, phonograph records, tape and wire recordings, maps, and globes.

6 Government publications.

THE PURPOSE OF RULES AND REGULATIONS

In order that all students will have an equal opportunity to use the library materials, certain rules and regulations are established in all libraries. These rules govern the kinds of materials which are circulated, the length of time they can be borrowed, the fines charged for overdue books, the use of library facilities—reading rooms, listening rooms, conference rooms, and other special areas—and the hours of service.

A part of the freshman orientation program in most colleges is a visit to the library. In many college libraries students are given a handbook which includes information about the physical arrangement of the library, the kinds of materials it provides, the classification system in use, the nature of the card catalog, the rules governing the use of the library, and the schedule of the hours the library is open.

The orientation visit to the library and the library handbook will have greater and more lasting meaning for the student who follows it with a personal survey of the library, fixing in his mind the arrangement and purposes of the several rooms, taking stock of the kinds of reference books which are provided and their location, and learning firsthand the many kinds of books, materials, and services which are available to him.

CHAPTER THREE

THE PARTS OF THE BOOK

IN order to understand and appreciate the importance, significance, and usefulness of each of the physical parts of a book, one needs only to recall the lack of aids to the reader in the early forms of the book. In the papyrus roll of antiquity the writing was in columns from right to left, without spaces or punctuation marks. The roll was usually untitled; thus it was identifiable only by the label or tag attached to the outside. This label was called *titulus* by the Romans, whence our word "title." The Greeks began the practice of writing from left to right and introduced some punctuation marks.

Medieval manuscripts began with the *Incipit,* "Here begins," and ended with the *Explicit,* "Here is unfolded." The punctuation marks and accents used as early as the eighth century were different from those we use today. There was some separation of words, but it was more a separation of phrases and groups of letters than of individual words. It was not possible to make quick or easy reference to those long parchment manuscripts. Initial letters, particularly those with miniatures illustrative of the text, were the chief guides to the subject matter of the medieval manuscript. The first works to appear in book (codex) form were those which were referred to most often: the Bible and the digests of laws. Bookbinding appeared with the codex.

In early handwritten and printed books, facts of authorship, title, and publication, if given at all, were placed in a separate statement called the colophon at the end of the text. In the first printed books the text was arranged in columns, and the words were written continuously without a break. Gradually, however, words were separated from each other within a line. Next came the division of words into sentences by means of punctuation marks. In the sixteenth century, Aldus Manutius, an outstanding Venetian printer and scholar, introduced a method of punctuation from which has evolved our modern conventional system. Most of the marks he introduced came from those used by the Greek grammarians, but some of them were given new meanings.

The first title pages, which appeared about 1463, gave title and author; in the 1470s the date of publication was added. Page numbers and running titles appeared at about the same time. The short title, comparable to our half-title page, came into use about 1480. The title page with author, title, and name and address of printer became common after 1520. Other parts of the book developed rapidly, and by the beginning of the eighteenth century, even the index was a common feature.

THE PARTS OF THE BOOK

The physical divisions of the book can be grouped as follows: (1) the binding, (2) the preliminary pages, (3) the text, and (4) the auxiliary or reference material.

The Binding The binding holds the leaves of the book together, protects them, and makes them easy to handle. It may be plain or decorated, and it may bear the author's name and the title. It has two important parts, the spine and the end papers.

The spine is the binding edge of the book and carries the brief title, the author's name, the publisher, and the call number if it is a library book.

The end papers are pasted to the covers to make them stronger; they may carry useful information, such as tables, maps, graphs, and rules.

The Preliminary Pages The preliminary pages precede the body of the book and include the flyleaves, the half-title page, the frontispiece, the title page, the dedication, the preface, the table of contents, lists of illustrative material, and the introduction.

The flyleaves are blank pages next to the end papers; they are the first and last leaves in the book.

The half-title page precedes the title page and serves as protection for it; it gives the brief title of the book and the series title if the book belongs to a series.[1]

The frontispiece is an illustration relating to the subject matter of the book; it precedes the title page.

The title page is the first important printed page in the book; it includes the following items:

1 The title; that is, the name of the work
2 The subtitle, a descriptive phrase which clarifies or explains the main title
3 The author's name and, usually, facts concerning his status, such as academic position, academic degrees, and the names of his other works
4 The name of the editor, if there is one
5 The name of the illustrator, or translator, if there is one
6 The name of the person who wrote the introduction, if other than the author
7 The edition[2] if it is other than the first
8 The imprint, which includes the place of publication, the publisher, and the date of publication

The back (verso) of the title page gives the date of the coypright[3] and the names of the copyright owners.

[1] A series is a number of separate works issued successively and related to each other in subject, form, authorship, or publication.

[2] An edition is the total number of copies of a book or other publication printed from one set of type at one time. A revised edition is a new edition in which the text of the original work has been changed or new material has been added. A revised edition will have a new copyright.

[3] Copyright is the exclusive right to publish, reproduce, and sell a literary or an artistic work. The period of copyright is twenty-eight years, with the privilege of renewal for a similar period.

The dedication page follows the title page and bears the name or names of the person or persons to whom the author dedicates the book.

The preface introduces the author to the reader and gives his reasons for writing the book; it indicates those for whom the book is intended, acknowledges indebtedness for services and assistance, and explains the arrangement, symbols, and abbreviations used, as well as any special features.

The introduction describes the general subject matter and plan of the book.[4]

The table of contents is a list of the chapters of the book with page numbers; it may be so detailed that it serves as an outline of the book.

The lists of illustrative material may include illustrations, maps, or tables.

The Text   The text is made up of the numbered chapters and constitutes the main body of the book.

The Auxiliary or Reference Material   The auxiliary or reference material follows the text and may include an appendix, a bibliography, a glossary, notes, and an index.

An appendix contains material referred to, but not explained, in the text.

A bibliography may be a list of the books which the author has used in writing his book, or it may be a list of materials which he recommends for further reading.

The glossary is a section which lists and explains all technical or foreign words not explained in the body of the book.

All footnotes, if they are not placed at the bottom of each page, may be placed in a section for notes. This section may contain explanations of certain passages in the text.

The index is a list of the topics discussed in the text, arranged alphabetically with page references. An index may have subdivisions of the topics and cross references.

Not all books have all the parts which have been discussed in the preceding paragraphs, nor do the parts always follow the order given in

[4] The introduction may be written by the author, by a person of importance who has encouraged the author to write the book, or by one who considers the book an important contribution. It may be an elaboration of the preface, or it may be the first chapter in the book.

this chapter. However, each part of the book is added because it contributes to the book's usefulness.

The binding holds the pages of the book together and makes them easy to handle and to use. If it is a beautiful binding, it will add to the aesthetic, as well as to the material, value of the book.

The title page provides most of the items included in a bibliographical description of the book: author, title, edition, and imprint. If the book is one of a series, the series title may be on the title page.

The table of contents serves as a brief outline of the content of the book and is useful in a search for material on a subject.

The preface and introduction, by indicating the purpose of the book, the audience to which it is addressed, and the treatment of the subject matter, will help the reader to know in advance whether or not the book will be useful to him for a given purpose.

The bibliography provides references to additional material on the subjects treated in the book.

The index is an aid in using the book because it points out the page location of small items discussed in it. The index of any book is useful to the person who is looking for material on a subject covered by that book.

Care in opening a book when it is new and careful handling of the book at all times will add to its years of usefulness and to the reader's enjoyment of it.

❧ PART TWO ❧

THE ORGANIZATION AND ARRANGEMENT OF LIBRARY MATERIALS

CHAPTER FOUR

CLASSIFICATION

CLASSIFICATION is the systematic arrangement of objects, ideas, books, or other items which have like qualities or characteristics into groups or classes. The "like" characteristics may be size, color, type, form, content, or some other feature.

HISTORICAL DEVELOPMENT OF THE CLASSIFICATION OF BOOKS

Ever since there have been books there has been the problem of organizing and arranging them so that they can be used easily and conveniently. Clay tablets were arranged on narrow shelves according to subject or type. Papyrus rolls were placed in clay jars or metal cylinders and labeled with a few key words describing their content. Parchment rolls were divided by author and title or by major subject or form groups and were placed in bins or on shelves. In medieval monasteries, manuscripts were classified as religious or secular, Latin or Greek; or they were divided according to subject matter, and all books on a subject were kept in the same chest. Books in medieval university libraries were divided according to the subjects taught and were arranged by size and accession on shelves or in chests. After the advent of printing, books were classified as manuscript books or printed books or as Latin, Greek, or Hebrew. In the college libraries of Colonial America, the organization was by location symbol—alcove 1, shelf A, book 6—with subject or language divisions within the alcoves.

Since the time of Aristotle, philosophers and nonphilosophers alike have been devising schemes for the classification of knowledge. In his *Advancement of Learning*, published in 1605, Sir Francis Bacon developed a plan for classifying knowledge into three large divisions: history, poetry, and philosophy; these large divisions were then subdivided into specific classes, with further subdivisions within the classes.

Thomas Jefferson adapted Bacon's plan for the classification of knowledge for use in his personal library at Monticello, and when he sold his library of 6,700 volumes to the United States to replace the Congressional Library which had been destroyed by the British in 1814, his classification system went along with it and was used by the Library of Congress until 1897.

When Melville Dewey, a student library assistant at Amherst College in 1872, decided to organize the contents of the college library, his first step was to develop a classification system. After studying the schemes for classifying knowledge which had been devised by Aristotle, Bacon, Locke, and other philosophers, as well as some recently published library classification schemes, he decided to group books according to subject matter. Like his predecessors, Dewey divided all knowledge into main classes which he subdivided into specific classes and into further subdivisions within each class, always proceeding from the general to the specific.

PURPOSES AND CHARACTERISTICS OF LIBRARY CLASSIFICATION SYSTEMS

The chief purpose of a classification system in a library is to provide a basis for organizing books and materials so that they can be found quickly and easily by those persons who use the library; it is also a means of bringing books on the same subject together so that they can be used easily and conveniently. Since ease of use is the basic concern, library classification schemes place materials in those categories from which they are most likely to be called for by those who need them. In addition, such schemes provide for the form of the material as well as for the subject matter; for example, dictionaries, encyclopedias, handbooks, periodicals, and other book forms have particular notations.

The first step in classifying according to subject is to arrange all knowledge into major classes, bringing together into one class the parts which are related and arranging the parts in some logical order, usually from the general to the particular. The several classes so formed constitute the classification scheme.

In order to be used, these classes must follow a definite and established plan or order so that they can be referred to again and again. Such a plan is called a schedule, with the classes and subdivisions within the classes arranged in logical order.

Each class of the schedule and each subdivision within each class must be given a symbol so that all the books in which a particular subject is discussed can be given the same notation and kept together on the shelves of the library. The symbols used are letters of the alphabet, Arabic numerals, or a combination of these.

Library classification systems follow the generally accepted ideas of what the major classes of knowledge are: philosophy, religion, science, history, language, literature, art, and so on. A general class number or letter is assigned to these large classes; for example, in the Dewey Decimal Classification System, 800 is Literature and 900 is History, and in the Library of Congress Classification System, P is Literature and D is History. Specific areas within the large classes are also given numbers: 930 is Ancient History, 973 is United States History, and 976.784 is History of Chicot County, Arkansas. The smallest number belongs to the largest subjects, and the longest numbers are assigned to the smallest or most specialized areas. Thus 600 is Technology (Applied Science), 620 is Engineering, and 629.134354 is Rocket Engineering.

In addition to a definite and established schedule of classes, there must be an index to all materials which are classified according to this schedule so that these materials can be found quickly and easily. The index to all of the classified materials in a library is the card catalog, which gives the location symbol for each publication. This location symbol is the call number, composed of the classification number and the book number (see pages 46–48).

Theoretically, a classification system should be so organized that material on any one subject can be found in only one place. Some subjects, however, have so many aspects, so many phases, so many contributing factors that it may not be possible to place all material relating to such a subject in only one class. For example, on a given subject, historical information may be found in the History class, economic data in Economics, sociological facts in Sociology, cultural information in Literature. Thus, in the story of books and libraries (Chapter One), material was found in every major class in the Dewey Decimal System:

1   The 000 class provided basic factual material on the story of books and libraries.

2   The 100 class gave the contributions of ancient and medieval philosophers to books and learning.

3   The 200 class was consulted for illustrative material on the Bible as a book and for information on the Hebrews, Aramaens, and Phoenicians.

4   The 300 class provided the social and economic background which made possible the rise of universities, the invention of printing, and the establishment of the first colleges in Colonial America.

5   The 400 class provided the story of writing and the alphabet.

6   The 500 class was consulted for archaeological findings.

7   The 600 class contributed the story of printing and the making of books.

8   The 700 class was the source of much illustrative material on the illumination of books, on miniatures, and on the graphic arts.

9   The 800 class gave the cultural influences on the development of books and libraries.

10 The 900 class identified geographical locations and historical events and provided biographical information on outstanding persons.

It is important to remember that even though books are classified according to the subject which is given the greatest emphasis, they may, to some extent, treat other subjects.

THE LIBRARY OF CONGRESS CLASSIFICATION SYSTEM

In 1897 the task of recataloging and reclassifying the Library of Congress collection was begun. The Library of Congress Classification System, which was developed in that process, combines letters of the alphabet and Arabic numerals; it provides for the most minute grouping of subjects through the combination of letters and numerals; it is designed for libraries with very large collections. The letters I, O, W, X, and Y are not used but are left for further expansion.

A brief outline of the Library of Congress Classification System follows:[1]

A	General Works—Polygraphy	L	Education
B	Philosophy—Religion	M	Music
C	History—Auxiliary Sciences	N	Fine Arts
D	History and Topography (except America)	P	Language and Literature
E–F	America	Q	Science
G	Geography—Anthropology	R	Medicine
H	Social Sciences	S	Agriculture—Plant and Animal Industry
J	Political Science	T	Technology
K	Law	U	Military Science
		V	Naval Science
		Z	Bibliography and Library Science

THE DEWEY DECIMAL CLASSIFICATION SYSTEM[2]

In the Dewey Decimal Classification System, Arabic numerals are used decimally to signify the various classes of subjects.

Dewey divided all knowledge, as represented by books and other

[1] From The Library of Congress, Subject Cataloging Division, *Outline of the Library of Congress Classification* (revised and enlarged ed. of "Outline Scheme of Classes"; Washington, D.C.: U.S. Government Printing Office, 1942).

[2] "Editor's Introduction," *Dewey Decimal Classification and Relative Index,* devised by Melville Dewey (16th ed.; Lake Placid, N.Y.: Forest Press, Inc., 1958), I, 5–12.

materials, into nine classes which he numbered 100 to 900. Materials too general to belong in a specific group—encyclopedias, dictionaries, newspapers, handbooks, and the like—he placed in a tenth class, which preceded the others as the 000 class. Each of the nine subject classes was organized as follows: The first of the ten divisions of every subject class was given to the general books in that subject; the remaining nine divisions were assigned to specific subject areas. The 800 class, Literature,[3] illustrates this general-to-particular organization.

800 Class, Literature (General Divisions[4])

800	Literature (in general)
801	Philosophy and theory (of literature)
802	Handbooks and outlines (of literature)
803	Dictionaries and encyclopedias (of literature)
804	Essays (on literature)
805	Periodicals (in the field of literature)
806	Organizations and societies (in the field of literature)
807	Study and teaching (of literature)
808	Collections (of literature)
809	History and criticism (of literature)

800 Class, Literature (Specialized Divisions)

810	American literature
820	English literature
830	German literature
840	French literature
850	Italian literature
860	Spanish literature
870	Latin and other Italic literatures
880	Classical and modern Greek
890	Other literatures

In 1876 Dewey's *A Classification and Subject Index for Cataloguing and Arranging the Books and Pamphlets of a Library* was published anonymously. Today about 96 per cent of the public libraries, 89 per cent of the college and university libraries, and 64 per cent of the special

---

[3] Printed by permission of Lake Placid Club Education Foundation, owner of copyright.

[4] The words in parentheses are the author's.

libraries in the United States follow Dewey's system.[5] It has been translated in whole or in part into more than thirteen languages and is now in the sixteenth edition.

The Dewey Decimal Classification System provides for the form as well as for the subject matter of the materials to be classified. The major form divisions are:[6]

01	Philosophy and theory	05	Periodicals
02	Handbooks and outlines	06	Organizations and societies
03	Dictionaries and encyclopedias	07	Study and teaching
		08	Collections and polygraphy
04	Essays and lectures	09	History and local treatment

The classes of the Dewey Decimal System, as listed in the Second Summary: Divisions, follow.

Second Summary: Divisions[7]

000	General works	200	Religion
010	Bibliography	210	Natural theology
020	Library science	220	Bible
030	General encyclopedias	230	Doctrinal theology
040	General collected essays	240	Devotional and practical
050	General periodicals	250	Pastoral theology
060	General societies	260	Christian church
070	Newspaper journalism	270	Christian church history
080	Collected works	280	Christian churches and sects
090	Manuscripts and rare books	290	Other religions
100	Philosophy	300	Social sciences
110	Metaphysics	310	Statistics
120	Metaphysical theories	320	Political science
130	Branches of psychology	330	Economics
140	Philosophical topics	340	Law
150	General psychology	350	Public administration
160	Logic	360	Social welfare
170	Ethics	370	Education
180	Ancient and medieval	380	Public service and utilities
190	Modern philosophy	390	Customs and folklore

[5] *Ibid.*, p. 6.

[6] *Ibid.*, p. 10. Printed by permission of Lake Placid Club Education Foundation, owner of copyright.

[7] *Ibid.*, p. 78. Printed by permission of Lake Placid Club Education Foundation, owner of copyright.

400	Language	700	The arts
410	Comparative linguistics	710	Landscape and civic art
420	English and Anglo-Saxon	720	Architecture
430	Germanic languages	730	Sculpture
440	French, Provençal, Catalan	740	Drawing and decorative arts
450	Italian, Rumanian	750	Painting
460	Spanish, Portuguese	760	Prints and print making
470	Latin and other Italic languages	770	Photography
480	Classical and modern Greek	780	Music
490	Other languages	790	Recreation
500	Pure science	800	Literature
510	Mathematics	810	American literature in English
520	Astronomy	820	English and Old English
530	Physics	830	Germanic literatures
540	Chemistry and allied sciences	840	French, Provençal, Catalan
550	Earth sciences	850	Italian, Rumanian
560	Paleontology	860	Spanish, Portuguese
570	Anthropology and biology	870	Latin and other Italic literatures
580	Botanical sciences	880	Classical and modern Greek
590	Zoological sciences	890	Other literatures
600	Technology	900	History
610	Medical sciences	910	Geography, travels, description
620	Engineering	920	Biography
630	Agriculture	930	Ancient history
640	Home economics	940	Europe
650	Business	950	Asia
660	Chemical technology	960	Africa
670	Manufactures	970	North America
680	Other manufactures	980	South America
690	Building construction	990	Other parts of the world

THE CALL NUMBER

A book is classified according to the subject matter it covers and is given the number in the classification schedule which stands for that subject. The class number for Ancient History is 930; since many books are written on that subject, and since all of them will be placed in the 930 class, it is necessary to have a means of distinguishing one book about ancient history from another book on the same subject. This distinction is made by assigning a *book number* (or author number) as well as a class number, using the initial of the author's last name plus Arabic numerals. The table from which the author number is taken was developed by C. A. Cutter about the same time that Dewey was devising his classification system. The Cutter table assigns certain numerals, used decimally, to letters of the alphabet in the order of the alphabet. Listed below is a group of letters of the alphabet with their numerical symbols from the *Cutter Three-figure Author Table:*[8]

B	1	C	Babe	115	Cado
Ba	11	Ca	Baber	116	Cae
Baak	111	Cab	Babi	117	Caffi
Baas	112	Cabl	Babn	118	Cagn
Babb	113	Cac	Babr	119	Cah
Babc	114	Cadd			

The class number for *Ancient History* by Allen Cable is 930; the book or author number from the sample Cutter table is C11. These two notations, 930 and C11, make up the call number of the book. The title of a publication may be represented in the call number by the first letter of the title, excluding articles. This letter, in lower case, is placed immediately following the book number and serves to distinguish between books on the same subject written by the same author. Thus the call number for *Ancient History* by Allen Cable is 930 C11a, whereas the call number for *A Survey of Ancient History* by Allen Cable is 930 C11s.

The arrangement of books on the shelves follows the outline of the classification system. Books with the following call numbers will appear on the shelves in this order:

338	338	338.095	338.1	338.1247	338.15
Am3a	H46s	B38m	Am3m	J13s	B21m

In some libraries, fiction and biography are not classified. Books of fiction may be given the designation F or Fic plus an author number from the Cutter table and arranged alphabetically on the shelves by author. An example is Fic B93s.

---

[8] Printed by permission of Ammi Cutter, owner of copyright.

Biography, instead of being given a class number, may be marked B and arranged in alphabetical order by the subject of the biography, as B C11.

Special symbols are sometimes added to the call number to indicate that the book is shelved in a particular location or that it is a particular kind of material. For example, the symbol R or Ref with the call number signifies that the book is a reference book and that it is located in the reference collection. J or C above or below the call number might mean that the book is in the children's collection. H.II. or a similar symbol with the call number may indicate that the book is one of a memorial gift collection which is kept together in one place.

The purpose of a classification system is to organize and arrange books and materials so that they can be found easily and quickly. Throughout the history of books and libraries, the most satisfactory method of classifying library materials has been by subject.

Before books can be placed in a subject group, all subject matter must be organized into major classes, and these major classes must be subdivided into many related classes. Each class must be assigned a notation symbol so that all books which cover a particular subject will have the same number. An index to all classed materials must be provided; this index is the card catalog.

An understanding of library classification systems in general, and of the one in use by a particular library, is essential to the effective use of that library.

The user must understand that a class number does not embrace all the materials on a given subject, that books are classified according to the subject which is given the greatest emphasis, and that he may find additional material on his subject in some or in all the major classes of the classification system.

The classification system provides an introduction to the generally accepted divisions of knowledge.

The classification schedule is an illustration of the process of limiting a subject, of proceeding from a large general subject to smaller specialized areas of that subject.

An understanding of the classification system and of the form divisions helps the user to locate quickly the books and materials in any reference room or in an open-shelf library. It enables him to go directly to that section of the library where books on a given subject are shelved and to locate easily the general books—dictionaries, encyclopedias, handbooks, and indexes—in a subject field.

THE CARD CATALOG

ORIGINALLY, the word "catalog" meant a list or an enumeration. It has come to mean a systematic or methodical arrangement of items in alphabetical or other logical order, with the addition of brief descriptive information such as price, size, and color. A library catalog, then, is a systematic listing of the books, and materials in a library with descriptive information about each one: author, title, edition, publisher, date, physical appearance, subject matter, special features, and location. It is an index to the contents of a library, just as the index of a book is a key to the contents of that particular book; it is the reader's chief means of discovering and locating material in a library.

GENERAL CHARACTERISTICS OF LIBRARY CATALOGS

The library catalog as we know it today had its beginnings in the lists which were carved or painted on the walls of the Sumerian and Egyptian temples, in the rough check lists and notebooks of the libraries of the early Middle Ages, and in the handwritten cards filed alphabetically in trays in the Harvard Library as early as 1869.

Some library catalogs today are in the form of printed books. Such printed catalogs are easy to handle and to duplicate, but they are soon out of date because new materials are constantly being added to the library collection.

Most library catalogs are on 3- by 5-inch cards, printed, typewritten, or mimeographed, and are filed alphabetically in trays. Other characteristics that library catalogs have in common are:

1   They provide aids for the user: labels on the outside and guide cards on the inside of the trays.

2   They have many cross references: a *see* reference refers from a heading that *is not* used to one that *is* used; a *see also* reference refers from a heading that *is* used to another that *is also* used.

Education—Colonies	Literature, Aesthetics
see	*see also*
Education, Colonial	Style, Literary
Literature—Anthologies	Education, Art
see	*see*
Anthologies	Art—Study and teaching
Education, Medieval	Literature—Evaluation
see also	*see*
Universities and colleges— Europe	Books—Reviews

3   The catalog cards in all library catalogs give the same kinds of information about books, in the same order: author, title, imprint, collation,[1] notes, subject headings, and other entries.

The chief function of the catalog is to make the total resources of the library fully and easily accessible to the user.

1   It points out the location of every book in the library by giving the location symbol, or call number.

2   It lists in one place, in alphabetical order, all books by a particular author or on a particular subject, regardless of their locations in the library.

[1] The collation indicates the number of volumes or pages, the number and kind of illustrations, and the size.

3   It provides several ways of finding materials, listing them by author, title, subject; by coauthor, translator, or illustrator, if there is one; and often by series, if the book belongs to a series.

There are several kinds of library catalogs, but few libraries have all of them.

1   A *subject* catalog is made up exclusively of subject cards.
2   An *author* catalog includes only the author or main-entry cards.
3   A *dictionary* catalog, which is the most common, has all cards— author, subject, title, and other entries—filed in one alphabet.

In some libraries the catalog is divided into two parts, with the author and title cards in one part and the subject cards in the other.

KINDS OF ENTRIES (CARDS) IN THE CARD CATALOG

An entry is a single listing of a publication. Most publications have two entries in the card catalog. (1) They are entered under author and (2) they are entered under title or subject. Most books other than fiction are listed under author and subject. In addition, books may be entered in the catalog under coauthor, editor, translator, and illustrator.

Author Card   The author card is the basic card and is called the main entry. It gives the following information, in the order listed:

1   The author's full name, inverted, the date of his birth, and the date of his death if he is not living
2   The title and the subtitle
3   The edition, if it is not the first
4   The coauthor, illustrator, translator
5   The imprint, which includes the place of publication, the publisher, and the date of publication
6   The collation, which includes the number of pages or volumes, the illustrative material, and the size of the book in centimeters
7   The series to which the book belongs, if it is one of a series
8   The subjects which are treated fully in the book
9   The full name and dates of the coauthor, translator, editor, or illustrator

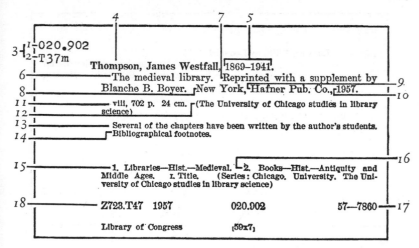

Figure 1 Author card or main entry: (1) class number; (2) author or book number; (3) call number; (4) author's name, inverted; (5) author's date of birth and death; (6) title of book; (7) edition; (8) place of publication; (9) publisher; (10) date of publication; (11) collation; (12) series note; (13) explanatory note; (14) bibliographical note; (15) subject heading (the subject treated fully); (16) another subject heading; (17) Library of Congress Catalog Card Number; (18) Library of Congress Classification.

The catalog card may give other pertinent information about the book, such as a note concerning the contents or the pages on which bibliography is located.

The author or main entry for a publication may be:

1 An individual
2 An individual who edits rather than writes the work
3 An institution
    a The U.S. Office of Education
    b The University of Chicago
4 A committee
    a Committee on Higher Education
    b Committee on the Teaching of English
5 A title or a publication
    a The Bible: Old Testament
    b The National Geographic Magazine

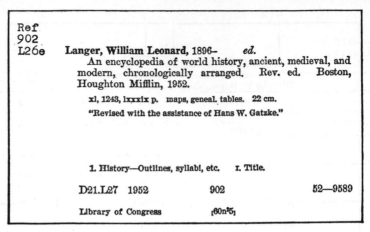

Ref
902
L26e   **Langer, William Leonard,** 1896–   *ed.*
An encyclopedia of world history, ancient, medieval, and
modern, chronologically arranged. Rev. ed.   Boston,
Houghton Mifflin, 1952.

xl, 1243, lxxxix p.   maps, geneal. tables.   22 cm.

"Revised with the assistance of Hans W. Gatzke."

1. History—Outlines, syllabi, etc.   i. Title.

D21.L27 1952   902   52—9589

Library of Congress   ₍60n²5₎

Figure 2   Editor as main entry.

Title Card   A title card is made for a book which has a distinctive
title. The title is typed at the top of the card in black, above the author's
name. If the title of the book is used as the author or main entry, there
will not be a title card in the catalog for that book.

Subject Card   There is no set number of subject cards for each
book; a subject card is made for every subject which is discussed fully in
the book. A subject card differs from all other types of entries in that the
subject is typed at the top of the card in red letters, or in black capital

Figure 3   A publication as author or main entry.

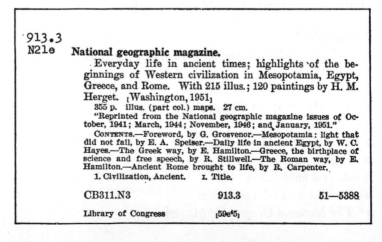

913.3
N21e   **National geographic magazine.**
Everyday life in ancient times; highlights ·of the be-
ginnings of Western civilization in Mesopotamia, Egypt,
Greece, and Rome. With 215 illus.; 120 paintings by H. M.
Herget. ₍Washington, 1951₎

355 p. illus. (part col.) maps. 27 cm.

"Reprinted from the National geographic magazine issues of October, 1941; March, 1944; November, 1946; and January, 1951."

CONTENTS.—Foreword, by G. Grosvenor.—Mesopotamia: light that
did not fail, by E. A. Speiser.—Daily life in ancient Egypt, by W. C.
Hayes.—The Greek way, by E. Hamilton.—Greece, the birthplace of
science and free speech, by R. Stillwell.—The Roman way, by E.
Hamilton.—Ancient Rome brought to life, by R. Carpenter.

1. Civilization, Ancient.   i. Title.

CB311.N3   913.3   51—5388

Library of Congress   ₍59e⁴5₎

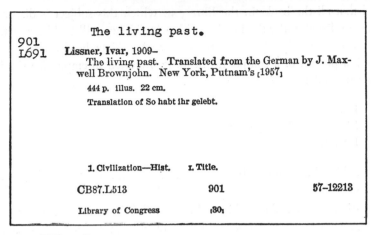

The living past.

901
L691   Lissner, Ivar, 1909–
            The living past. Translated from the German by J. Max-
        well Brownjohn. New York, Putnam's [1957]

            444 p. illus. 22 cm.

            Translation of So habt ihr gelebt.

            1. Civilization—Hist.   ɪ. Title.

            CB87.L513   901   57–12213

            Library of Congress   [30]

Figure 4   Title card.

letters. No other kind of heading is typed in this manner. The remainder
of the card is an exact duplicate of the main-entry card.

Subject headings describe the contents of a book and therefore
indicate to the reader the usefulness of that book for his purpose. Subject
headings are logical and uniform and are used consistently throughout
the card catalog. The subject headings used for one book on a given subject will be used for *all* the books in the library which deal fully with that
same subject. If the reader is searching for material on "libraries," he will

Figure 5   Subject card.

BOOKS--HISTORY--ANTIQUITY AND MIDDLE AGES

091
K42b   Kenyon, *Sir* Frederic George, 1863–
            Books and readers in ancient Greece and Rome, by Fred-
        eric G. Kenyon ... Oxford, The Clarendon press, 1932.

            vi p., 1 l., 136 p. illus., plates, facsims. (1 double)   18½ cm.

            This book is the outcome of a course of three lectures delivered at
        King's college, University of London, in March 1932.—Pref.

            CONTENTS.—I. The use of books in ancient Greece.—II. The Papyrus
        roll.—III. Books and reading at Rome.—IV. Vellum and the codex.—
        Appendix. Illustrative passages from Latin authors.

            1. Books—Hist.—Antiquity and middle ages. 2. Books and reading.
        3. Manuscripts (Papyri) 4. Parchment.   ɪ. Title.

            Z112.K38   091   33—1934

            Library of Congress   [a53j†2]

find that all the books in the library in which this subject is discussed fully are listed under the heading "libraries." They will be filed together in the catalog, alphabetically by author. A subject heading may be a word, a phrase, or a compound heading, inverted to emphasize the important words:

> Literature
> Literature—Bibliography
> Literature, Modern

The subject heading may be determined by the form of the work (American poetry—Collections) or by location (Education—U.S.), or it may be a location subdivided by subject (France—Politics and government).

A knowledge and understanding of subject headings is essential to the efficient use of the catalog. If the student knows the author or title of a book, it is relatively simple, if the library has the book, to find it in the catalog. If, however, the student's assignment is to find material *on a subject,* he must have an understanding of the nature of subject headings—how they are determined and how they are phrased—in order to know how to look for his topic in the card catalog. For example, if his topic is "social life in the United States," he will look in the catalog for U.S.—Social life and customs. If the topic is "compulsory education," he will look for Education, Compulsory.

Examples of other topics and their subject headings are:

Topic	*Subject heading*
The American novel	American fiction—History and criticism
The history of contemporary England	Great Britain—History—Twentieth century
The history of music	Music—History
The American Revolution	U.S.—History—Revolution
The government of France	France—Politics and government

Careful reading of the subject headings listed on each card will result in the discovery of other subjects under which material on the topic under study can be found. If the topic is "books and libraries," the

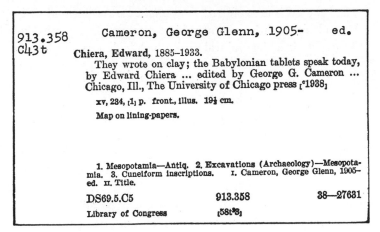

913.358
C43t

Cameron, George Glenn, 1905-   ed.

Chiera, Edward, 1885–1933.
    They wrote on clay; the Babylonian tablets speak today,
by Edward Chiera ... edited by George G. Cameron ...
Chicago, Ill., The University of Chicago press [ᶜ1938]
        xv, 234, [1] p. front., illus. 19½ cm.
    Map on lining-papers.

    1. Mesopotamia—Antiq. 2. Excavations (Archaeology)—Mesopota-
mia. 3. Cuneiform inscriptions.   i. Cameron, George Glenn, 1905–
ed. ii. Title.

DS69.5.C5   913.358   38—27631

Library of Congress   [58t⁶8]

Figure 6   *Editor as added entry.*

student will be able to go from the heading Books to the heading Books—
History, to Libraries—History, to Writing—History, and so forth.

Other Entries   If a book has a joint author or an important editor,
illustrator, or translator, a card is made for each one. The name of the
person is typed at the top of the card, above the author's name, in black.
These cards are called added entries.

When a title card and an author card are made for each of the
stories, plays, or essays in an anthology, each card is called an *analytical*

Figure 7   *Analytical entry.*

913.3
N21e

        Daily life in ancient Egypt.

        Hayes, William C.

            Daily life in ancient Egypt. (In
        National Geographic Magazine. Every-
        day life in ancient times. 1958.
        pp. 71-168.)

entry, and the cards are referred to as *analytics.* Author and title cards may be made for each important subject discussed in a yearbook or for each biographee in a biographical work which includes several persons.

The catalog card stands for the book it describes, and intelligent interpretation of the information on the catalog card is almost equivalent to seeing the volume for which it is made. The main card gives the items which appear on the title page of the book. In addition, it describes the book as to size, number of pages, and kinds and amount of illustrative material. It indicates whether the book has a bibliography, and it may list the contents. It gives the subject or subjects treated in the book in the order of emphasis, the first subject heading listed being the one which is treated most completely. In many cases, it is possible to select or to reject a book by reading and understanding the catalog card.

ARRANGEMENT OF CARDS IN THE CATALOG

Rules for arranging cards in the catalog are adopted by each library. There are some variations, but in general these practices are followed:

1　Alphabetical arrangement is word-by-word rather than letter-by-letter. Examples of word-by-word and letter-by-letter arrangement are:

Word-by-word	*Letter-by-letter*
Fort Dodge	Fort Dodge
Fort Erie	Forte
Fort Knox	Fort Erie
Fort Smith	Forth
Fort Wayne	Fortification
Forte	Fort Knox
Forth	Fortress
Fortification	Fort Smith
Fortress	Fortunate
Fortunate	Fort Wayne

2　Abbreviations are filed as if they were spelled out: St. is filed Saint, Mr. is filed Mister, and so on.

3　Names beginning with Mc and M' are arranged as if they were spelled Mac.

4 Definite and indefinite articles at the beginning of titles and other headings are ignored.
5 Historical subheadings are filed in chronological order.
6 Books *by* a person are filed before books *about* him.
7 The latest edition of a book is filed before the first edition.

An example of the simplest form of arranging catalog cards, following these practices, is listed below:

The ABC of lettering	McHenry, William
The A cappella chorus book	Machines
Aaron, Daniel, editor	McNeill, Richard
The Abbey theatre	Mr. Mack
Ability	Monetary fund
Ability—Testing	100 days
Accent on teaching	Only a rose
Accents on opera	St. Augustine
Education—History	School days
Educational psychology	Shaw, George Bernard, 1856–
Literature	1950 (as author)
Literature—Dictionaries	SHAW, GEORGE BER-
Literature—History	NARD, 1856–1950[2] (as subject)
	U.S.—History—Colonial period
	U.S.—History—Revolution
	U.S.—History—Civil War

[2] As subject, Shaw, George Bernard, 1856–1950, would be typed in red or in black capital letters, just as other subject headings are typed.

PART THREE

GENERAL REFERENCE MATERIALS

✻ CHAPTER SIX ✻

REFERENCE MATERIALS

THE word "reference" comes from the verb refer, which means to turn to for aid or information. Thus any person or thing referred to for these purposes is a reference. A book which is consulted for aid or information on a topic, a theme, an event, a person, a date, a place, or a word is a reference book. In this sense, the entire library is a reference collection, because it was selected, organized, and arranged for study and reference.

> This library will . . . constitute in itself, as it were, a single gigantic superbook of encyclopedic information in thousands and thousands of volumes. Through its shelf arrangements, catalogs, subject indexes, and bibliographies the seeker for information can find what he desires.[1]

However, in any library there are some books which are consulted more frequently than others for certain kinds of information; there are

[1] Pierce Butler (ed.), *The Reference Function of the Library* ("The University of Chicago Studies in Library Science"; Chicago: The University of Chicago Press, 1943), p. 11.

books which, because of their organization and arrangement, lend themselves to quick and easy use; and there are other publications which were planned and written to be *referred to* for pieces of information rather than to be read completely. In most libraries these kinds of materials are brought together in one room or area and constitute what is called the reference collection, the reference room, or the reference department. The use of these materials is restricted to the library. Questions may be answered completely from the resources in the reference collection, or a given source may only indicate other books and materials which the information seeker must consult to secure the full answer to his question.

It should be clear, then, that the reference collection, room, or department is not a separate library within itself but is only one of the many parts of the total library that the student will use in his search for material.

DEFINITION AND CHARACTERISTICS OF REFERENCE BOOKS

The term "reference book" has come to mean a specific kind of publication which has been planned and written to be consulted for items of information, rather than read throughout. It contains facts that have been brought together from many sources and organized for quick and easy use, either in an alphabetical or chronological arrangement or by the use of detailed indexes and numerous cross references.

If a student is to use reference books effectively and advantageously, he must develop a facility in using them independently. He acquires this facility as he learns what reference books are, the kinds that are available, the types of questions each kind will answer, and how each book is arranged.

TYPES AND CLASSES OF REFERENCE BOOKS

There are two types of reference books: (1) those which contain the needed information, such as dictionaries, encyclopedias, handbooks, biographical dictionaries, atlases, and gazetteers; and (2) those which tell the user where the information can be found, such as indexes, bibliographies, and directories.

These two types of reference books are of two classes, general and specialized, the latter referred to in this text as "subject" reference materials.

General Reference Books General reference books are those which are broad in scope, not limited to any single subject, but useful for all, or at least for many, subject areas. The kinds of general reference books, according to their form and the material which they include, are dictionaries, encyclopedias, indexes, yearbooks, handbooks, almanacs, biographical dictionaries, directories, atlases, gazetteers, and bibliographies.

Each kind of reference book is designed to do specific things. Theoretically, a given reference book does the specific things it is planned to do better than any other reference book can do them; thus it should be consulted *first* for the kind of information it covers, even though other reference books may include some of the same information. For example, a dictionary or an encyclopedia may give information about a geographical location, but a gazetteer, which is designed for the sole purpose of providing information about geographical names and places, is the first place to look for information concerning a geographical location.

The kinds of general reference books, the purposes they serve, and examples of each kind are listed below:

1 A dictionary provides information about words—meaning, derivation, spelling, pronunciation, syllabication, usage, and current status.

a *Webster's New International Dictionary of the English Language*

b *Funk & Wagnalls New Standard Dictionary of the English Language*

2 An encyclopedia is concerned with subjects. It gives an overview of a topic, including definition, description, background, and bibliographical references.

a *Encyclopedia Americana*

b *Encyclopaedia Britannica*

3 An index points out *where* information can be found. There are indexes to articles which appear in periodicals and there are indexes

to articles, essays, poems, and other writings which appear in collected works.

   a   *Readers' Guide to Periodical Literature*
   b   *Essay and General Literature Index*

4   A yearbook, often called an annual, presents the events of the past year in brief, concise form.

   a   *The American Yearbook*
   b   *Britannica Book of the Year*

5   A handbook, literally a small book which can be held conveniently in the hand, provides miscellaneous items of information. It may also be called a miscellany, a manual, a companion, or a compendium.

   a   *Brewer's Dictionary of Phrase and Fable*
   b   *The Book of Days*

6   An almanac, originally a projection of the coming year by days, months, holidays, and weather forecasts, is the name now given to a collection of miscellaneous facts and statistical information.

   a   *The World Almanac and Book of Facts*
   b   *Information Please Almanac*

7   A biographical dictionary is a collection of sketches of varying lengths about the lives of individuals, arranged alphabetically by surname.

   a   *Who's Who*
   b   *Dictionary of American Biography*

8   A directory lists the names and addresses of persons, organizations, or institutions. It may provide other pertinent information, such as the purposes, the dues, and the officers of organizations.

   a   *N. W. Ayer & Son's Directory of Newspapers and Periodicals*
   b   *The World of Learning*

9   An atlas is a volume of maps, plates, or charts, with or without explanatory text.

   a   *Hammond's Ambassador World Atlas*
   b   *Goode's World Atlas*

10   A gazetteer is a volume which provides geographical information and data about places.

   a   *Columbia-Lippincott Gazetteer of the World*
   b   *Webster's Geographical Dictionary*

11   A bibliography is a list of books and other materials which have some relationship to each other. The materials listed are described as

to author, title, publisher, price, and number of pages. In some bibliographies the materials are evaluated.

a   Cumulative Book Index
b   Bibliography of Bibliographies

Subject Reference Books   Subject reference books are those in which the material is devoted to a specific subject area, such as literature, art, or history. In most subject fields, there are the same kinds of reference books as there are in the general field. Subject reference books are discussed in Chapters Fifteen to Twenty-two.

DETERMINING THE USEFULNESS OF A REFERENCE BOOK

The usefulness of a reference book for a particular purpose may be determined by answering some basic questions.

1   Are those who produced the subject matter—the editorial staff as listed on the title page or in the preliminary pages—specialists in their fields, as indicated by the academic or by some other position which they hold?
2   Is the usefulness of the subject matter of the book under consideration affected by time, and if so, is this book out of date?
3   Does the book attempt to cover more than it is possible to handle in a work of this size?
4   Is the book arranged for quick and easy use, with adequate index and cross references?
5   Does it provide text alone, or does it include illustrative material as well? Is the illustrative material well chosen?
6   Is the treatment of material, as stated in the preface,
    a   Simple for the layman?
    b   Technical for the expert?
    c   Scholarly for the scholar?
7   Is there any indication of bias in the treatment of material?
8   Does the book provide bibliographies, and are they up-to-date?
9   Is the print clear and legible?

10 What kinds of questions will this book answer:
   a Factual?
   b Statistical?
   c Historical?
   d Current information?
11 What subject areas are emphasized:
   a Science?
   b Literature?
   c Social science?

CHOOSING A REFERENCE BOOK

In choosing a reference book to answer a given question most conveniently and effectively, it is necessary to understand the nature of the question and to know the usefulness of the various reference books in answering given questions. First analyze the question, then decide which reference book or books provide the kinds of information it requires.

1 What kind of information is needed to answer the question:
   a A definition of terms?
   b Statistical information?
   c An exhaustive explanation or discussion?
   d A brief summary?
2 In what subject area does the question belong:
   a History, economics, geography?
   b An area touching several subject fields?
3 What factors affect the question:
   a Date?
   b Location?
   c Economic conditions?
   d Historical events?
4 What kind of reference book is needed:
   a A general dictionary for definitions?
   b A subject dictionary for specialized terminology?
   c An encyclopedia for an overview or a summary?

d A periodical article for current information?

e A yearbook for statistics?

f A combination of several reference books?

USING REFERENCE BOOKS

In order to use any reference book intelligently and efficiently, it is necessary to read the preliminary pages which explain its distinguishing features. These features include:

1 The plan followed in the organization and presentation of material:
   a Alphabetical, word-by-word or letter-by-letter
   b Chronological
   c Topical, with detailed indexes giving page numbers or some other kind of numerical reference, such as the number of a poem in an anthology or the number of an entry
2 The symbols and abbreviations used in the text
3 The diacritical marking or the phonetic transcription used to indicate pronunciation

In the chapters immediately following, each kind of general reference book will be discussed, with emphasis upon its usefulness for a particular purpose.

CHAPTER SEVEN

DICTIONARIES

> . . . sur l'utilité des Dictionnaires. Le public est assez convaincu qu'il n'y a point de livres qui rendent de plus grands services, ni plus promptement, ni à plus de gens que ceux-là [les Dictionnaires][1]

THE earliest dictionaries were those in which the meanings of the words of one language were given in the words of another. Among the clay tablets recovered from the ruins of the Sumerian civilization are dictionaries which give Sumerian words with their Semitic-Assyrian meanings. The word *dictionarius,* meaning a collection of words, was first used in the English language ca. 1225 as the title of a collection of Latin terms. Several Latin-English dictionaries, as well as English and other modern language dictionaries, appeared before the end of the sixteenth century. In the seventeenth century, the name dictionary was gradually given to works explaining English words in English.

The first general and comprehensive dictionary of the English lan-

[1] "Preface," Antoine Furetière (comp.), *Dictionnaire Universel* (A La Haye et à Rotterdam: Chez Arnout et Reinier Leers, 1691), I, 1.

guage was the *Universal Etymological English Dictionary* by Nathan Bailey, published in 1721, which gave pronunciation and authority for pronunciation but only very brief definitions.

Samuel Johnson's *A Dictionary of the English Language*, which appeared in 1755, was designed to list all "good" words in the language with their "proper" meanings. There were many quotations to illustrate the uses of words, and these illustrative quotations have been repeated by makers of dictionaries since that time. Johnson's *Dictionary* was used in England and America until 1828, when it was superseded by Noah Webster's *American Dictionary of the English Language*. *Webster's New International Dictionary of the English Language*, which we use today, is the successor to the 1828 work.

The next important English dictionary was the *New English Dictionary on Historical Principles*. Sir James Murray, as editor, began the task of publishing this scholarly ten-volume work in 1878. It was not completed until 1928. Reissued in 1933, with some corrections and additions, as the *Oxford English Dictionary*, it is an example of the application of the historical method to words, giving the origin, meaning, and historical development of English words in general use now or at any time since 1150.

CHARACTERISTICS OF DICTIONARIES

Following the pattern established by the distinguished *American Dictionary of the English Language* and the *Oxford English Dictionary*, the dictionary today is, first of all, a collection of words in which each word is treated as to pronunciation, derivation, usage, meaning, and syllabication. In addition, the dictionary may give synonyms, antonyms, illustrative quotations, maps and plates, biographical facts, and geographical information. Thus a dictionary may be a combination of word book, gazetteer, thesaurus, biographical dictionary, and encyclopedia.

Because most dictionaries are arranged alphabetically for convenience of reference, the word "dictionary" has come to mean any alphabetical arrangement of words or topics. A collection of items of information in a special subject area, arranged in alphabetical order, is often called a dictionary. There are dictionaries of psychology, education, philosophy, music, mathematics, and many other subjects, as well as dictionaries of dates, events, battles, plants, and sports. In fact, dictionaries of subjects and of things surpass in number those of words or language.

When only a few words, a small part of those belonging to a subject, are given, or when these words are only partially explained, the work is a *vocabulary*. When it is a list of explanations of technical words and expressions in some particular subject or in a book, it is a *glossary*.

DETERMINING THE USEFULNESS OF A DICTIONARY

The primary purpose of any dictionary is to answer questions about words. The usefulness of a dictionary is determined by the way in which it answers them. In order to use a dictionary most effectively, it is necessary to understand what it has to offer and in what manner the material is presented. The user must learn the kinds of dictionaries and the distinguishing characteristics of each kind, in order to decide which one or ones will answer a given question most completely and most satisfactorily.

In judging the usefulness of a dictionary, consider these points:

1   What part of the language does the dictionary include? Slang, dialect, obsolete, and technical words, as well as standard words?
2   What period of the language does it cover?
3   Is grammatical usage given?
4   Are plurals, verb tenses, and participles spelled?
5   Is syllabication indicated?
6   In what way is pronunciation shown? If diacritical marks are used, are they explained?
7   Are the definitions clear?
8   Are the definitions given in order of historical or current usage?
9   Is the etymology of the word given?
10   Is illustrative material—quotations, maps, pictures, charts—used? If so, is it adequate and apropos?
11   Does it give synonyms and antonyms, and are they explained?
12   Are abbreviations and symbols explained?
13   Is encyclopedic information, that is, biography, geographical and historical facts, and like material included?

14 Is the dictionary easy to use?

15 How does it compare with other dictionaries on each of these points?

Many of the questions listed above will be answered as one uses the various dictionaries; other answers will be found in the preface and introduction of each dictionary. Making a dictionary is a very complicated and technical task, and any good dictionary will have a large staff of specialists as editors. These editors will explain the steps they have followed in making the dictionary. In order to use a dictionary most efficiently, the student must examine the table of contents, the preface, and the introductory material of the dictionary when consulting it for the first time.

KINDS OF DICTIONARIES

Dictionaries can be divided into (1) general word dictionaries, which provide over-all information such as pronunciation, derivation, syllabication, meaning, etc., about the words of a language, and (2) dictionaries which have to do with certain aspects of language such as etymology, synonyms and antonyms, slang, colloquialisms, dialect, and usage.

General word dictionaries are (1) unabridged, that is, complete, or (2) abridged, that is, reduced in content but retaining the features of the unabridged work. They include both English language and foreign language dictionaries.

Dictionaries which are concerned with certain aspects of language are discussed in Chapter Nineteen, Language (Philology).

REPRESENTATIVE DICTIONARIES

General Word Dictionaries—Unabridged

Craigie, Sir William A., and Others (eds.). *A Dictionary of American English on Historical Principles.* 2d ed. Chicago: University of Chicago Press, 1960. 4 vols. Follows the plan of the *Oxford English Dictionary;* continues the story of the English language into Colonial America and to the end of the nineteenth century; indicates which words originated in America; does not include slang and dialect.

Funk & Wagnalls New Standard Dictionary of the English Language. New York: Funk & Wagnalls Company, 1959. Includes all live words of the language; gives current meaning first; provides pronunciation, spelling, etymology; includes many technical terms, illustrative quotations from newspapers and periodicals, and geographical entries; has an appendix of foreign words and phrases.

Murray, Sir James Augustus Henry, and Others (eds.). *The Oxford English Dictionary.* Being a corrected reissue, with an introduction, supplement, and bibliography, of *A New English Dictionary on Historical Principles.* London: Oxford University Press, 1933. 12 vols. and supplement. Presents the historical development of each word introduced into the English language since 1150, giving the date it was introduced and the uses which have survived; each meaning illustrated with a quotation from literature; gives pronunciation, etymology, inflectional forms, and synonyms.

Webster's New International Dictionary of the English Language. 2d ed. Springfield, Mass.: G. & C. Merriam Company, 1959. Gives definitions in historical sequence; features a pronouncing gazetteer and biographical information; includes slang, dialect, obsolete, and technical words; provides pronunciation, etymology, inflectional forms; indicates British pronunciation; includes foreign words and phrases in the main vocabulary. In the new 3d ed., 1961, archaic words and phrases are omitted and a conscious effort is made toward popularization.

Figure 8 Excerpts from entries in Webster's New International Dictionary: (1) *vocabulary entry;* (2) *pronunciation—Webster phonetic alphabet, diacritical marks;* (3) *part of speech;* (4) *etymology—*(5) *Middle English,* (6) *from,* (7) *Old French,* (8) *Latin,* (9) *Greek;* (10) *etymology cross references—cf.* (*compare*) *implying that there is a relationship between the words;* (11) *heavy-faced Arabic numerals used to number definitions which are very different in meaning;* (12) *a definition with separate meanings numbered;* (13) *heavy-faced letters used when the meanings can be grouped easily;* (14) *technical and scientific meanings arranged in alphabetical order;* (15) *see reference for information of great importance or essential to an understanding of the meaning;* (16) *vocabulary entry;* (17) *etymology of verb form;* (18) *part of speech;* (19) *and* (20) *inflectional forms;* (21) *verb form;* (22) *example illustrating the meaning;* (23) *illustrative quotation from literature;* (24) *verb form.* (*From* Webster's New International Dictionary of the English Language. 2d ed. *Springfield Mass.:* G. & C. Merriam Company, *Publishers of the Merriam-Webster Dictionaries, copyright 1959.*)

cir′cle (sûr′k′l), *n.* [ME. *cercle,* fr. OF. *cercle,* fr. L. *circulus,* dim. of *circus* circle; akin to Gr. *krikos, kirkos,* circle. Cf. CIRCULATE, CIRCUS, CIRCUM-, SEARCH.] **1. a** A closed plane curve such that all of its points are equidistant from a point within called the *center;* a ring; a circumference. The area of a circle may be found by multiplying the square of the radius by the number π (3.14159265). **b** The plane surface bounded by such a curve.

2. A halo, as around the moon.

3. Of a heavenly body: **a** Formerly, the sphere in which it supposedly revolved; now, the orbit; also, the period of revolution. **b** The sphere or orb.

4. Something having in general a circular form; as: **a** A ring or circlet. **b** A crown; diadem; coronet. **c** A circular group of persons; a ring. **d** A circus ring. **e** A group of tiers of seats in a theater. **f** A sheet or plate whose contour forms a circle (sense 1).

5. Compass; circuit. "In the *circle* of this forest." *Shak.*

6. A series ending where it begins, and repeating itself.

Thus in a *circle* runs the peasant's pain. *Dryden.*

7. A set or series of parts connected to form a whole; a system; cycle; round; as, a *circle* of pleasures, of sciences.

8. A company conceived to be assembled about a central point of interest, or bound by a common tie; a class or division of society; a coterie; a set.

The *circle* of his acquaintance widened. *Macaulay.*

9. Circuit of action or influence; realm. Cf. SPHERE.

10. A territorial division or district; specif.: **a** In the Holy Roman Empire, any of the ten principalities or provinces which had seats in the Diet. **b** [G. *kreis.*] In modern Germany, a division for local government; specif., in Prussia, Thuringia, etc., a subdivision of a province; in Württemberg, Bavaria, etc., a larger administrative district, corresponding in general to the English county. **c** [It. *circondario.*] In Italy, a subdivision of the province.

11. *Archaeol.* A group of stones in a ring, as at Stonehenge.

12. *Astron.* An instrument of observation, the graduated limb of which consists of an entire circle. When mounted, as formerly, on a heavy pier or wall in an observatory, for measuring zenith distances, it is called a *mural circle;* when mounted with a telescope on an axis and turning in Y's, in the plane of the meridian, a *meridian,* or *transit, circle;* when mounted so as to turn to any azimuth, a *vertical circle;* when involving the principle of reflection, like the sextant, a *reflecting circle;* and when that of repeating an angle several times around the graduated limb, a *repeating circle.* See TRANSIT INSTRUMENT.

13. *Bookbinding.* See ROLL, *n.*

14. *Gymnastics.* Any feat or exercise in which the body or a part of it describes a circle.

15. *Logic.* A form of reasoning in which the conclusion is unwarrantably assumed in the grounds or hypotheses from which the reasoning proceeds; begging the question.

16. *Naut.* A circle of latitude or longitude.

17. *Petroleum.* Any circular steel rack on which a jack is operated for setting up or breaking tool joints, as drilling tools in oil-well drilling.

18. *Weaving.* A flat piece sometimes used as a substitute for a swivel shuttle in hand looms and power looms.

☞ COMBINATIONS and PHRASES are:

circle-branching, *adj.*	circle finisher	circle shears
circle cutter	circle setter	circle squarer
circle driller	circle-shearing, *adj.* circle-squaring, *adj.*	

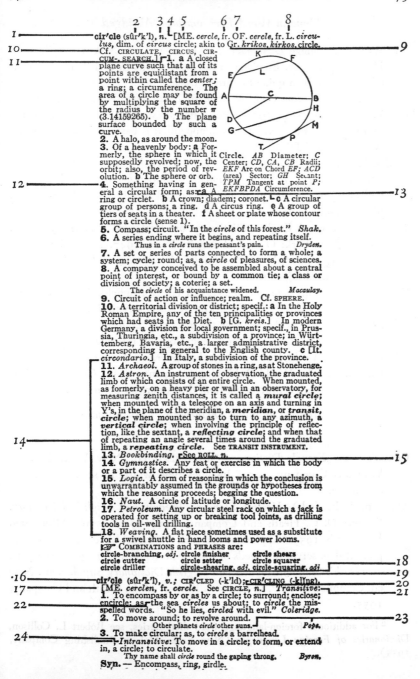

Circle. *AB* Diameter; *C* Center; *CD, CA, CB* Radii; *EKF* Arc on Chord *EF; ACD* (area) Sector; *GH* Secant; *TPM* Tangent at point *P; EKFBPDA* Circumference.

cir′cle (sûr′k′l), *v.;* CIR′CLED (-k′ld); CIR′CLING (-klĭng). [ME. *cerclen,* fr. *cercle.* See CIRCLE, *n.*] *Transitive:* **1.** To encompass by or as by a circle; to surround; enclose; encircle; as, the sea *circles* us about; to *circle* the misspelled words. "So he lies, *circled* with evil." *Coleridge.*

2. To move around; to revolve around.

Other planets *circle* other suns. *Pope.*

3. To make circular; as, to *circle* a barrelhead.

Intransitive: To move in a circle; to form, or extend in, a circle; to circulate.

Thy name shall *circle* round the gaping throng. *Byron.*

Syn. — Encompass, ring, girdle.

General Word Dictionaries—Abridged

The American College Dictionary. Newly revised ed. New York: Random House, Inc., 1957. Emphasizes the basic words in each field of knowledge; aims to be a guide to current usage.

Funk & Wagnalls New College Standard Dictionary. New York: Funk & Wagnalls Company, 1956. Underlines stressed syllables; gives population statistics and abbreviations in appendix; is based on the unabridged *New Standard Dictionary.*

Funk & Wagnalls Standard Dictionary of the English Language. International ed. New York: Funk & Wagnalls Company, 1958. Includes "established" words, technical and specialized terminology, slang, foreign phrases, and names.

The Shorter Oxford English Dictionary on Historical Principles. 3d ed. revised. New York: Oxford University Press, 1947. 2 vols. An authorized abridgment of the *Oxford English Dictionary;* includes features of that work in abridged form.

Webster's New Collegiate Dictionary. 6th ed. Springfield, Mass.: G. & C. Merriam Company, 1960. Based on *Webster's New International Dictionary,* 2d ed.; seeks to meet the needs of college students and the general reader; does not include encyclopedic information.

Webster's New World Dictionary of the American Language. College ed. Cleveland: The World Publishing Company, 1959. Gives definitions in mid-twentieth-century style from the American point of view.

Foreign Language Dictionaries[2]—Bilingual

FRENCH

Cassell's New French Dictionary. 5th revised ed. New York: Funk & Wagnalls Company, 1951. Includes new words in science, art, and commerce.

Mansion, J. E. (ed.). *Heath's Standard French and English Dictionary.* Boston: D. C. Heath and Company, 1934–1939. 2 vols. (Reprinted 1959 with 1955 *Supplement* in each volume.) A dictionary of the present day; serves the needs of those who read the foreign newspapers.

————. *Heath's Standard French and English Dictionary Supplement.* New ed. Compiled by R. P. L. Ledésert. Boston: D. C. Heath and Company, 1955.

---

[2] For additional foreign-language word dictionaries, see Robert L. Collison, *Dictionaries of Foreign Languages* (New York: Hafner Publishing Company, 1955).

GERMAN

Barker, M. L., Homeyer, H., and Carr, C. T. (comps.). *The Pocket Oxford German Dictionary*. London: Oxford University Press, 1951. Designed for general use.

Betteridge, Harold T. (ed.). *The New Cassell's German Dictionary: German-English, English-German*. Based on the editions by Karl Breul, completely revised and reedited. New York: Funk & Wagnalls Company, 1958. Includes technical words, geographical and proper names; emphasizes current usage.

GREEK

Edwards, Gerald Maclean (ed.). *English-Greek Lexicon*. London: Cambridge University Press, 1912. (Reprinted, 1938.) Useful for ancient Greek.

ITALIAN

Rebora, Piero, and Others (comps.). *Cassell's Italian-English, English-Italian Dictionary*. London: Cassell & Co., Ltd., 1958. A general dictionary of the Italian language; includes colloquialisms and new words, as well as obsolete words and words found in the classics.

Hoare, Alfred (ed.). *Italian Dictionary*. 2d ed. London: Cambridge University Press, 1925. Serves as a reference dictionary for literary use; includes quotations, phrases, idioms.

LATIN

Simpson, D. P. (ed.). *Cassell's New Latin Dictionary: Latin-English, English-Latin*. Completely revised. New York: Funk & Wagnalls Company, 1960. Includes new material; useful for beginning students.

RUSSIAN

Müller, Vladimir Karlovich (ed.). *English-Russian Dictionary*. 6th ed. New York: E. P. Dutton & Co., Inc., 1959. A general dictionary of the Russian spoken language, is modern and up-to-date. (See Smirnitsky for Russian-English volume.)

Segal, Louis (ed.). *New Complete English-Russian Dictionary*. 3d ed. London: Percy Lund, Humphries & Co., Ltd., 1958. Includes new words, technical terms, idioms, colloquialisms.

Smirnitsky, Aleksandr Ivanovich. *Russian-English Dictionary*. 3d ed. revised and enlarged. Under the editorship of O. S. Akhmanova. New York: E. P. Dutton & Co., Inc., 1959. Gives general coverage; is up-to-date. (See Müller for English-Russian volume.)

SPANISH

Cuyás, Arturo (ed.). *Appleton's New English-Spanish and Spanish-English Dictionary*. Revised ed. New York: Appleton-Century-Crofts, Inc., 1953. 2 vols. Includes idioms and specialized terms; gives particular emphasis to usage in the United States and Latin America.

Hinojosa, Ida Navarro (ed.). *New Revised Velázquez Spanish and English Dictionary*. Chicago: Follett Publishing Co., 1959. An exhaustive revision; presents thousands of new terms and idiomatic expressions of general use, including terminology of business, current events, technology, and science.

Peers, Edgar Allison, and Others (comps.). *Cassell's Spanish Dictionary: Spanish-English, English-Spanish*. New York: Funk & Wagnalls Company, 1960. Gives due emphasis to the Spanish of Latin America.

CHAPTER EIGHT

ENCYCLOPEDIAS

OF all the reference books in any library, perhaps none is more revered than the encyclopedia; not without reason, for the encyclopedia has a long noble history and a heritage of high and lofty purpose. Since ancient times, it has been the aim and desire of encyclopedia makers to bring together into one work *all* human knowledge.

The first encyclopedias were works of a single author, designed to summarize the knowledge and thinking of his time. Aristotle produced a large number of encyclopedic treatises. The *Historia Naturalis* of Pliny the Elder, dating from A.D. 77, has been called the first encyclopedia because of its method of compilation. It is the oldest encyclopedia in existence.[1]

In general, the encyclopedias of the Middle Ages were devoted to

[1] Translated into English by Philemon Holland in 1601, the *Historia Naturalis* was the standard authority for many centuries on the subjects it included: physics, geography, ethnology, physiology, zoology, botany, medical information, minerals, and art. Forty-three editions were published before 1536. It is now being published in the Loeb Classical Library in ten volumes.

one or another of the sciences, but Isadore, Bishop of Seville, attempted to cover every branch of knowledge in his work, which is sometimes called the "Encyclopedia of the Middle Ages."

In 1630 the first modern encyclopedia (the first work to be given the title encyclopedia) was published in Switzerland by Johann Heinrich Alsted. French contributions to encyclopedia making in the seventeenth century were the *Grand Dictionnaire* of Louis Moréri and the *Dictionnaire Historique et Critique* of Pierre Bayle.

English encyclopedias began with the two-volume *Cyclopaedia* of Ephraim Chambers in 1728, which became the model for all encyclopedias that followed. Translated into French, it provided the working basis for *L'Encyclopédie du XVIIIᵉ Siècle*, which was edited by Diderot and d'Alembert from 1751 to 1772, with all of the savants of France as members of the editorial staff.

The *Encyclopaedia Britannica* was first published in Edinburgh in 1771 in three volumes as a dictionary of the arts and sciences. The next edition, in ten volumes, added history and biography. Other and larger editions followed, including the scholarly ninth and eleventh editions. In 1920 it was acquired by Sears, Roebuck & Company, which gave it to the University of Chicago in 1943.

Encyclopedia editing in the United States began with the publication of the *Encyclopedia Americana* in 1829. The *New International Encyclopedia,* which introduced the journalistic style into encyclopedia writing, appeared in 1884.

By derivation, encyclopedia means instruction in the circle of arts and sciences—considered by the Greeks to be essential to a liberal education. Diderot envisioned his *Encyclopédie* as an "immense *dépôt* in which he would collect and arrange all human knowledge." Guizot (1828) saw the encyclopedia as a "vast intellectual bazaar where the results of all the works of the human spirit are offered to whosoever stops to satisfy his curiosity" and as a work which "places a host of ideas and deeds at the door of a host of men who never dreamed of them, who, without encyclopedias, would never have heard of them!"[2]

Today, as it has from the beginning, the encyclopedia purports to be a repository of information on all branches of knowledge, presenting

---

[2] François Pierre Guillaume Guizot, quoted in "Encyclopédie," *Grand Dictionnaire Universel du XIXᵉ Siècle Français* (1870), VII, 516.

the basic general principles and the most essential details of each of the arts and sciences. It gives an overview of each subject, with definition, description, explanation, history, current status, statistics, and bibliography. It is organized, usually in alphabetical arrangement, for rapid and easy use.

A work of this magnitude calls for the most careful planning and editing and the most experienced writers. Reputable publishers of encyclopedias spare no expense in making their works authoritative and accurate.

Because of the amount of work involved, it is not possible to revise an encyclopedia every year. Therefore, the chief means of keeping an encyclopedia up-to-date is by publishing an annual supplement or yearbook. In addition to publishing yearbooks, most of the major encyclopedia publishers have programs called "continuous revision." This means that their editorial specialists are always at work on the subjects for which they are responsible and that each time the encyclopedia is reprinted (not revised) certain articles are brought up-to-date. For example, those members of the editorial staff of a major encyclopedia who are responsible for writing the article on rockets have acquired much new information since the encyclopedia was published in 1959. The encyclopedia will be reprinted in 1962 from the 1959 plates. The 1962 edition will be the same as the 1959 edition, except that the article on rockets, and certain other articles, will be completely rewritten. Thus with every printing some new material is added, and in time, the entire encyclopedia will appear in a new and revised edition. This is continuous revision.

There are encyclopedias written for scholars and educated adults, there are some addressed to laymen, and there are others designed for young people and children. In each of these encyclopedias, the basic factual material may be the same; they differ in style of writing, in amount of additional material included, and in manner of presentation.

Although the primary purpose of an encyclopedia is to present information on all branches of knowledge,[3] each encyclopedia has certain

[3] The name encyclopedia is given also to a work designed to present information on all phases of one particular branch of knowledge. This kind of encyclopedia is usually referred to as a *subject* encyclopedia, as distinguished from a *general* encyclopedia which covers all branches of knowledge.

strong points; for example, the *Encyclopedia Americana* is strong in science, technology, and literature; the *Encyclopaedia Britannica* in art, literature, and the biological sciences; the *World Book* in readability (each article having been written for age and/or grade levels); and *Compton's Pictured* Encylopedia in illustrative material.

CHOOSING AN ENCYCLOPEDIA

Encyclopedias are of two types:

1 The dictionary type treats subjects under many specific alphabetically arranged headings.
2 The monographic type presents its subjects under large general headings with many subdivisions. The monographic encyclopedia requires a comprehensive index and many cross references to locate small topics within the long articles.

The usefulness of an encyclopedia depends upon the extent to which it fulfills its stated purposes. In order to decide which encyclopedia can most satisfactorily provide material on a given subject, the student must become acquainted with each encyclopedia as to:

1 Its authoritativeness
   a Is the publisher well known and reputable?
   b Is the work dependable, as evidenced by an editorial staff of specialists in each field of knowledge?
2 Its purpose
   a What is the editor attempting to do?
   b For whom is the work intended?
     (1) Scholars?
     (2) Laymen?
     (3) Young people or children?
       (*a*) Is it planned to supplement the school or college curriculum?
       (*b*) Is it written on grade or age levels?
3 Its scope
   a Is it comprehensive in coverage?

   b Is it limited to one branch of knowledge?

4 Its up-to-dateness

   a Is it a new work?

   b Is it based on an old edition of the same title or of another title?

   c Is the material in the articles, including statistics, maps, and charts, out-of-date?

   d Are the bibliographies adequate and up-to-date?

      (*1*) Are they references for further reading on the subject?

      (*2*) Are they the sources used in writing the articles?

      (*3*) Do they follow each article, or are they collected into a single volume?

5 Its strong points

   a What subject areas are emphasized?

   b What features are superior to those in other encyclopedias?

6 Its physical make-up

   a Does the physical make-up, that is, the size of the volumes, the kind of paper, the type, the headings, and the lettering on the spine, add to the ease of use?

   b Is the illustrative material adequate and suitable to the text?

Some of these questions can be answered by reading the preliminary pages in each encyclopedia; others will be answered as the student uses the several encyclopedias.

USING AN ENCYCLOPEDIA

In using an encyclopedia for the first time, it is important to read the preface carefully in order to determine:

1 The organization of the material

   a Are there short articles on small subjects?

   b Are there long articles on large, general subjects?

2 The arrangement

   a Is it alphabetical letter-by-letter or word-by-word?

   b Is it topical?

3 The kind of index provided

    a Is there a detailed index which points out small subjects within the long articles?

    b Is there an index to each volume or a single index for the entire work?

4 The kinds of aids-to-the-reader

    a Is pronunciation indicated? If so, what system is followed?

    b Are cross references provided?

    c Are abbreviations and symbols explained?

The outstanding features of the general encyclopedias listed below are given in the annotations.

REPRESENTATIVE ENCYCLOPEDIAS

General Encyclopedias

The Encyclopedia Americana. New York: Americana Corporation, 1961. 30 vols. A scholarly work which includes short articles on small subjects, as well as long articles; gives the history of each century, information on American cities and towns, evaluations of literary and musical compositions, pronunciation of difficult words; provides cross references.

Encyclopaedia Britannica. Chicago: Encyclopaedia Britannica, Inc., 1961. 24 vols. Monographic in style, this scholarly work provides a complete index and many cross references.

Collier's Encyclopedia. New York: P. F. Collier & Son Corporation, 1961. 20 vols. Emphasizes modern subjects; includes material to supplement the curricula of college and secondary school.

Columbia Encyclopedia. 2d ed. New York: Columbia University Press, 1950. (*Supplement,* 1959.) Desk-type, has short, clear, concise articles.

Compton's Pictured Encyclopedia and Fact-index. Chicago: F. E. Compton & Company, 1961. 15 vols. Emphasizes the visual approach to a subject; provides graded articles.

The Lincoln Library of Essential Information. Revised ed. Buffalo, N.Y.: The Frontier Press Company, 1961. Divided into twelve areas of knowledge which are subdivided into chapters; is limited to essential information in these areas; has an alphabetical index.

The World Book Encyclopedia. Chicago: Field Enterprises Educational

Corporation, 1961. 18 vols. Written for grade and age levels; gives pronunciation and many cross references.

Foreign Encyclopedias

Bol'shaia Sovetskaia Entsiklopediia. 2d ed. Moscow: Sovetskaia Entsiklopediia, 1949–1958. 51 vols. Sponsored by the Soviet government; is international in scope.

Enciclopedia Italiana di Scienze, Lettere ed Arti. Rome: Instituto della Enciclopedia Italiana, 1929–1937. 35 vols. Provides long articles, many bibliographies, illustrations of all kinds, biography; illustrations for travel and art subjects most notable.

Brockhaus' Konversations-Lexikon. Der Grosse Brockhaus. Weisbaden: F. A. Brockhaus, 1952–1958. 12 vols. A model for encyclopedias in other languages; has frequent revisions.

Enciclopedia Universal Illustrada Europeo-Americana. Barcelona: Epasa, 1905–1933. 70 vols., with 10-volume supplement and a 1-volume appendix. *Suplemento Anual.* 1934– . Comprehensive in coverage; gives Spanish and Spanish-American biography and geographical names.

Grand Larousse Encyclopédique. Paris: Librairie Larousse, 1960– . 10 vols. (In progress.) A dictionary as well as an encyclopedia; covers contemporary subjects.

Larousse, Pierre Athanase. *Larousse du XXᵉ Siècle.* Paris: Larousse, 1928–1933. 6 vols. Has brief, illustrated articles.

❧ CHAPTER NINE ❧

INDEXES

THE word "index" comes from the Latin word *indicare*, which means to point out. Thus an index does not provide the information which is sought; it *indicates* where it can be found.

The index of a book points out the page or pages on which certain information can be found. The card catalog, which is made up of individual catalog cards, is an *index* to the materials in a library. Each catalog card indicates, by means of a call number, the location of a book or other kind of material. The catalog card may give the pages on which certain material can be found in a given book; for example, the card may have the notation, Bibliography: p. 210–212.

In addition to card catalogs and the indexes of books, three other kinds of indexes are needed by the student who seeks material on a particular subject: (1) indexes to literature appearing in periodicals, (2) indexes to materials appearing in newspapers, and (3) indexes to literature appearing in collections or anthologies.

PERIODICALS

Periodicals appeared in the sixteenth century soon after the invention of printing. They began as pamphlets, grew into a series of related pamphlets, and by the seventeenth century had taken on the characteristics of our modern periodicals. Throughout the eighteenth century, the word "periodical" was used chiefly as an adjective, e.g., periodical literature, periodical publication. By the end of that century the term was applied to all regularly issued publications except newspapers.

The word "journal" originally meant a daily newspaper or publication; it has since come to mean any publication which contains news or material of current interest in any particular field.

The historical meaning of the word "magazine," deriving from the Arabic *makhāzin*, was storehouse. The first publication in English with the word "magazine" in the title was the *Gentlemen's Magazine*, founded in London in 1731 and planned as a kind of repository for news, essays, and other outstanding and interesting pieces of literature. The word "magazine" referred at first to content only; it now includes form also, and means a collection of miscellaneous stories, articles, essays, poems, and other material, including illustrations, appearing at regular intervals. Since magazines appear periodically—weekly, monthly, bimonthly, or quarterly—they are often referred to as periodicals. In fact, the words "periodical," "journal," and "magazine" are generally used interchangeably.

The first magazine in America was published on February 13, 1741, when Andrew Bradford issued his *American Magazine, or a Monthly View of the Political State of the British Colonies*. Three days later, Benjamin Franklin published his *General Magazine, and Historical Chronicle, for All the British Plantations in America*. Both periodicals carried the publication date of January, 1741. Bradford's magazine lasted three months; Franklin's, six months. Several other magazines were published before 1775, but none survived the Revolution. Magazine publishing began again in 1779.[1]

From these meager beginnings, magazine publishing has grown un-

[1] Frank Luther Mott, *A History of American Magazines, 1741–1850* (Cambridge, Mass.: Harvard University Press, 1938), I, 2–8 and 24.

til now more than 7,000, including general-interest magazines, trade journals, vocational and recreational periodicals, and professional journals, are published in the United States.[2] A certain number of issues, usually covering six months or a year, constitute a volume. Some magazines publish an index for each volume, but many others do not provide an index of any kind.

The search for information on any subject must include the examination of material which appears in periodical publications. The importance of this material cannot be overemphasized.

1 The most recent material on a subject, especially in the fields of science, technology, statistics, politics, and economics, will be found in a periodical.

2 Subjects too new, or even too obscure or too temporary, to be covered by books are treated in periodicals.

3 The trend of interest or opinion at any given period is traced easily in periodical literature, the current issues giving contemporary information and the old issues giving a record of past ideas, problems, and accomplishments.

4 Books, or parts of books, often appear first in periodicals, before they are published as separate volumes.

5 Professional literature is supplemented by periodicals which keep the teacher, the scientist, the doctor, the economist, the lawyer, and the members of other professions up-to-date.

The importance of periodicals in supplementing information found in books is recognized by school and college accrediting agencies in their requirement that periodicals be included in the libraries of all schools under consideration for accreditation.

Periodical literature can be divided into two classes, general and professional. A general periodical is not limited to one area of interest but touches many interest areas. Examples are *Harper's Magazine, Life,* and *The Saturday Evening Post.* A professional periodical—usually called a professional journal—consists of articles on subjects of concern to a particular branch of knowledge, which are usually written by mem-

---

[2] James Playsted Wood, *Magazines in the United States* (2d ed.; New York: The Ronald Press Company, 1956), p. 326.

bers of the profession. Examples are *College English, Journal of Geography, American Journal of Psychology,* and *American Historical Review.*

PERIODICAL INDEXES

It would not be possible to make use of the countless pieces of information in periodicals without the aid of indexes. Even the indexes to each volume, when they are provided, may not bring to light all the important topics discussed. To aid the researcher in the use of periodicals, there are indexes to periodical literature. The function of an index to periodical literature is to point out the location of the topics discussed in the periodicals covered by the index. In carrying out this function, the index lists not only the large, general subjects treated, but also the various subdivisions of each subject; it indicates where material can be found on each of the several phases of a subject. For example, for purposes of indexing, the subject Literature includes the following subdivisions:[3]

Literature	Literature, Religious
Literature—Appreciation	Literature and art
Literature—Criticism	Literature and history
Literature—Philosophy	Literature and music
Literature—Social aspects	Literature and philosophy
Literature—Technique	Literature and politics
Literature, Ancient	Literature and science
Literature, Medieval	Literature and social problems
Literature, Modern	Literature as a profession

This detailed breakdown of a subject and the innumerable cross references which are provided are valuable aids to the student who is trying to choose a subject for a research paper, or who is trying to narrow and restrict a subject which he has chosen.

Each of the indexes to periodical literature covers a group of periodicals of a certain kind—general, scientific, educational, business, and so

[3] Adapted from *International Index,* April, 1956–March, 1957 (New York: The H. W. Wilson Company, 1957), pp. 404–405.

on. The list of periodicals covered is given in the front of each issue of the index. In general, one index does not include periodicals which have been covered by another index. Note the absence of duplication in the references given for the subject "civilization" in the excerpts from *Readers' Guide to Periodical Literature, Education Index,* and *International Index* (Figures 9, 10, and 11), which cover approximately the same period of time. It is necessary, therefore, to consult several indexes in order to locate the several kinds of periodicals which can be of help in answering a question.

Figure 9   Excerpts from Readers' Guide to Periodical Literature: (1) *Sir Winston Churchill as subject;* (2) *and* (3) *titles of articles about Sir Winston Churchill;* (4) *articles on "civil uniforms" are listed under this heading;* (5) *an excerpt from President Eisenhower's address can be found in the* Bulletin of Atomic Science, *volume 15, page 366, November, 1959;* (6) *title of the book;* (7) *editor of the book;* (8) *location of a review of the book,* Whitehead's American Essays in Social Philosophy, *edited by A. H. Johnson, reviewed by Y. H. Krikorian in the* Nation, *volume 189, pages 384–386, November 21, 1959;* (9) *subheading under "Civilization," i.e., Civilization—History;* (10) *author of the review of the book,* Muqaddimah; (11) *subheading under "Civilization," i.e., Civilization—Preservation of records.* (Readers' Guide to Periodical Literature. *New York: H. W. Wilson Company, December 10, 1959, p. 21.*)

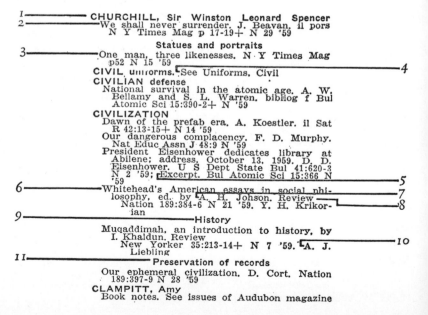

1——————CHURCHILL, Sir Winston Leonard Spencer
2———————We shall never surrender. J. Beavan. il pors
        N Y Times Mag p 17-19+ N 29 '59

        Statues and portraits
3——————One man, three likenesses. N Y Times Mag
        p52 N 15 '59
  CIVIL uniforms. See Uniforms, Civil ———————————4
  CIVILIAN defense
     National survival in the atomic age. A. W.
     Bellamy and S. L. Warren. bibliog f Bul
     Atomic Sci 15:390-2+ N '59
  CIVILIZATION
     Dawn of the prefab era. A. Koestler. il Sat
     R 42:13-15+ N 14 '59
     Our dangerous complacency. F. D. Murphy.
     Nat Educ Assn J 48:9 N '59
     President Eisenhower dedicates library at
     Abilene; address, October 13. 1959. D. D.
     Eisenhower. U S Dept State Bul 41:620-3
     N 2 '59; Excerpt. Bul Atomic Sci 15:366 N
     '59 ———————————————————————————————5
6——————Whitehead's American essays in social phi-——7
        losophy, ed. by A. H. Johson. Review ———
        Nation 189:384-6 N 21 '59. Y. H. Krikor-——8
9—————————————————ian
                    ——————History
  Muqaddimah, an introduction to history, by
     I. Khaldun. Review
     New Yorker 35:213-14+ N 7 '59. A. J.———10
     Liebling
11——————— Preservation of records
  Our ephemeral civilization. D. Cort. Nation
     189:397-9 N 28 '59
  CLAMPITT, Amy
     Book notes. See issues of Audubon magazine

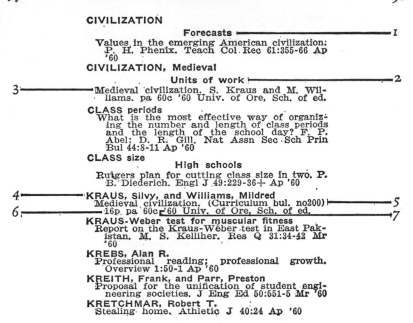

CIVILIZATION
Forecasts ━━━━━━━━━━━━ 1
Values in the emerging American civilization.
P. H. Phenix. Teach Col. Rec 61:355-66 Ap
'60

CIVILIZATION, Medieval
Units of work ━━━━━━━━━ 2
3 ━━━━━Medieval civilization. S. Kraus and M. Williams. pa 60c '60 Univ. of Ore, Sch. of ed.

CLASS periods
What is the most effective way of organizing the number and length of class periods and the length of the school day? F. P. Abel; D. R. Gill. Nat Assn Sec Sch Prin Bul 44:8-11 Ap '60

CLASS size
High schools
Rutgers plan for cutting class size in two. P. B. Diederich. Engl J 49:229-36+ Ap '60

4 ━━━━KRAUS, Silvy, and Williams, Mildred
Medieval civilization. (Curriculum bul. no200) ━━━ 5
6 ━━━━16p. pa 60c '60 Univ. of Ore, Sch. of ed. ━━━ 7

KRAUS-Weber test for muscular fitness
Report on the Kraus-Weber test in East Pakistan. M. S. Kelliher. Res Q 31:34-42 Mr '60

KREBS, Alan R.
Professional reading; professional growth. Overview 1:50-1 Ap '60

KREITH, Frank, and Parr, Preston
Proposal for the unification of student engineering societies. J Eng Ed 50:551-5 Mr '60

KRETCHMAR, Robert T.
Stealing home. Athletic J 40:24 Ap '60

Figure 10   Excerpts from Education Index: *(1) subheading under "Civilization,"
i.e., Civilization—Forecasts; (2) subheading under "Civilization, Medieval," i.e.,
Civilization, Medieval—Units of Work; (3) title of the publication by S. Kraus and
M. Williams; (4) full names of the coauthors named in 3; (5) series to which
the publication belongs; (6) facts about the publication—16 pages, paperback;
(7) name of publisher and date of publication.* (Education Index. New York: The
H. W. Wilson Company, May, 1960, pp. 14, 35.)

The location of a periodical article is given by volume, page, and date
of issue. In general, each article is listed under author and subject, with
complete information under the author entry.

Not all periodical indexes use both forms of listing. Some indexes
include a title entry; others index by subject only.

Some indexes point out only certain kinds of articles appearing in
periodicals, such as book reviews, bibliographies, or biographies.

In using a periodical index, as in using any other reference book, it
is necessary to understand the system of indexing, the kinds of articles
covered, the arrangement of items, and the method of abbreviating.

Determining the Usefulness of a Periodical Index   The usefulness
of a periodical index depends upon several factors:

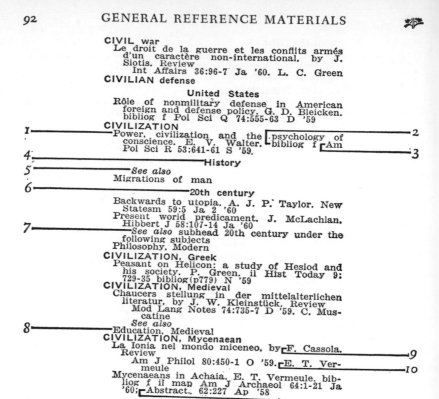

CIVIL war
Le droit de la guerre et les conflits armés
d'un caractère non-international, by J.
Siotis. Review
    Int Affairs 36:96-7 Ja '60. L. C. Green
CIVILIAN defense

United States
Rôle of nonmilitary defense in American
foreign and defense policy. G. D. Bleicken.
bibliog f Pol Sci Q 74:555-63 D '59
CIVILIZATION
    Power, civilization and the psychology of
    conscience. E. V. Walter. bibliog f Am
    Pol Sci R 53:641-61 S '59.
                                    History
            See also
Migrations of man
                        20th century
Backwards to utopia. A. J. P. Taylor. New
    Statesm 59:5 Ja 2 '60
Present world predicament. J. McLachlan.
    Hibbert J 58:107-14 Ja '60
            See also subhead 20th century under the
    following subjects
Philosophy, Modern
CIVILIZATION, Greek
Peasant on Helicon: a study of Hesiod and
    his society. P. Green. il Hist Today 9:
    729-35 bibliog(p779) N '59
CIVILIZATION, Medieval
Chaucers stellung in der mittelalterlichen
    literatur, by J. W. Kleinstück. Review
    Mod Lang Notes 74:735-7 D '59. C. Mus-
    catine
            See also
Education, Medieval
CIVILIZATION, Mycenaean
La Ionia nel mondo miceneo. by F. Cassola.
Review
    Am J Philol 80:450-1 O '59. E. T. Ver-
    meule
Mycenaeans in Achaia. E. T. Vermeule. bib-
    liog f il map Am J Archaeol 64:1-21 Ja
    '60; Abstract., 62:227 Ap '58

Figure 11 Excerpts *from* International Index: (1) *title of the article by E. V.
Walter;* (2) *the article has bibliographical footnotes;* (3) *it can be found in the*
American Political Science Review, *volume 53, pages 641–661, September, 1959;*
(4) *subheading under "Civilization,"* (5) *see also reference for the subject,*
Civilization—History; (6) *subheading under "Civilization";* (7) *see also reference*
for Civilization—Twentieth century, meaning that additional material on this
subject can be found under Philosophy, Modern—Twentieth century; (8) *see also*
reference for Civilization, Medieval; (9) *author of the book La Ionia nel mondo*
miceneo; (10) *author of the review of the book in 9, located in the* American
Journal of Philology, *volume 80, pages 450–451, October, 1959;* (11) *an abstract*
of the article "Mycenaeans in Achaia" appeared in volume 62, American Journal
of Archaeology, *April, 1958, page 227.* (International Index. New York: The
H. W. Wilson Company, March, 1960, p. 29.)

1 The number and kind of magazines covered by the index
2 The inclusion of books or parts of books
3 The period of time covered in the index—when it began and whether
   or not it is still being issued

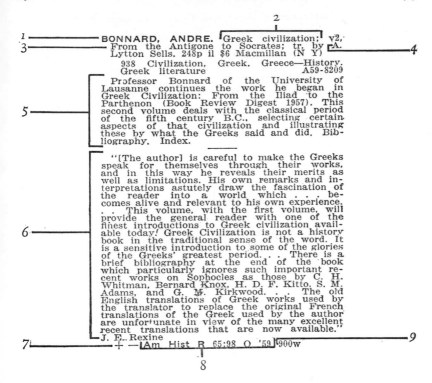

Figure 12 Excerpt from Book Review Digest: (1) author's name; (2) title of the entire work; (3) title of vol. 2 of Greek Civilization: From the Antigone to Socrates (4) translator of vol. 2; (5) annotation of From the Antigone to Socrates by the editors of Book Review Digest; (6) digest of a review by J. E. Rexine; (7) this review is both favorable and unfavorable; (8) this review is in the American Historical Review, volume 65, page 98, October, 1959; (9) the review has 900 words. (Book Review Digest. New York: The H. W. Wilson Company, January, 1960, p. 12.)

4 The completeness of the indexing of any periodical—all articles or only certain types of articles

5 The fullness of the information given—author, title, volume, page, date—as well as information about bibliographies and illustrations

6 The method of indexing—by subject as well as by author and title

7 The frequency of issue—bimonthly, monthly, quarterly, less often

8 Ease of use

Choosing and Using a Periodical Index In order to choose the right index for a particular problem, it is necessary to analyze the question:

1 What is the nature of the question?
  a Does it concern a topic or a person too new to be discussed in books?
  b Is it a topic so limited in appeal that it does not receive treatment in a book?
  c Is it a topic which is treated in a book but about which more recent information is needed?
  d Is it a topic which would be clarified by the discussions in one or more periodicals?
2 In what area does the problem belong?
  a History
  b Literature
  c Education
  d General
3 Which of the periodical indexes covers the literature of the area in question?
4 What years are involved, and which indexes cover those years?
5 Is an article from a general periodical, an article from a professional journal, or an article from each kind required?

Some useful indexes to periodical literature are listed below. The outstanding features of each index are given with the bibliographical entry; other features are shown in the tables at the back of the book.

Biography Index. New York: The H. W. Wilson Company, 1946– .
  (Quarterly; cumulated annual volumes are replaced by three-year permanent volumes.) The only index which gives birth and death dates and occupation or profession of each person listed; includes an index by profession; indexes biographical material in periodicals covered by the H. W. Wilson Company indexes; indexes books and parts of books; international in coverage, indicates nationality of persons who are not American; provides cumulative indexes which add to the ease of use.

Book Review Digest. New York: The H. W. Wilson Company, 1905– .
  (Monthly, except February and July; annual cumulations.) Indexes reviews of current books appearing in periodicals; gives author, title, pages, price, publisher, date, and descriptive note about each book in-

cluded; may give excerpts from reviews; indicates favorable or un-favorable trend of reviews by plus or minus sign; has title and subject index to books included.

Catholic Periodical Index. Villanova, Pa.: Catholic Library Association, 1930– . (Quarterly; two-year cumulations.) An author and subject index to a selected list of Catholic periodicals published mainly in the United States, Canada, England, and Ireland; notes articles written from the Catholic viewpoint elsewhere.

Nineteenth Century Readers' Guide, 1890–1899. New York: The H. W. Wilson Company, 1944. 2 vols. Author and subject index to fifty-one leading periodicals published in the 1890s; records authorship of many articles which were originally published anonymously.

Poole's Index to Periodical Literature, 1802–1907. Boston: Houghton, Mifflin Company, 1891. (Reprinted 1938 by Peter Smith, New York.) Indexes by subject only about 470 English and American periodicals chiefly of a general nature; fiction, poems, and plays are indexed by first important word of title; includes book reviews; was the first of the periodical indexes.

Readers' Guide to Periodical Literature. New York: The H. W. Wilson Company, 1900– . (Semimonthly from September to June, monthly during July and August; two-year cumulations.) Indexes more than 100 periodicals of a general nature; follows closely the publication date of the periodicals with semimonthly issues; gives author and title of article, name, volume, and date of periodical, number of pages; illustrations, bibliography, maps.

Abridged Readers' Guide to Periodical Literature. New York: The H. W. Wilson Company, 1935– . (Monthly except June to August.) For schools and small public libraries; indexes about thirty-five magazines; permanent volumes cover approximately two-year periods.

NEWSPAPERS

Newspapers developed from the seventeenth century broadside, which was a single large page printed on one side only. These early newspapers were issued weekly, or biweekly, and were sometimes called news-pamphlets or news-books.

Corantos was the name given to the periodical news-pamphlets is-sued between 1621 and 1641 to provide news of foreign countries. The *diurnalls,* or news-books, gave the domestic news during the years from 1641 to 1645.

The biweekly *Oxford Gazette* was the first newspaper in the modern sense to be published in England. It appeared in November, 1665. A year later it was renamed the *London Gazette;*[4] it is still issued twice a week, not as a newspaper, however, but as a record of official matters.

The first newspaper published in America appeared in Boston in 1690 and was called *Publick Occurrences, Both Foreign and Domestick;* there was only one issue. The first newspaper to be published for a continuous period was the *Boston News-Letter,* which appeared in April, 1704. The first daily newspaper in America was the *Pennsylvania Packet and General Advertiser,* established in Philadelphia in 1784. The *New York Times,* founded in 1851, was, from the very beginning, one of the world's outstanding newspapers. In the twentieth century there have been such developments as chains of newspapers, tabloids, and syndicated news services.

In addition to news events, the modern newspaper provides other features, such as illustrations; book reviews; articles on education, art, music, drama, and recreation; literary contributions; and biographical features.

The function of newspapers now, as in the past, is to keep the reader up-to-date on events. They are valuable sources of information on questions of the day and on trends of opinion in the past. They provide a contemporary history of any given modern period.

NEWSPAPER INDEXES

It is necessary to use indexes and bibliographies in order to make the most effective use of newspapers. There is no general index to newspapers comparable to the periodical indexes, but since all newspapers publish news items at about the same time, the date of the event will serve as the needed clue. An index of dates, like that in the *Americana*

---

[4] The word "gazette" probably came from *gazzetta,* the Italian name for a small Venetian coin which was the price charged (in the sixteenth century) for a copy of a newssheet or for permission to read it (*Oxford English Dictionary,* IV, 88–89).

Annual, or an index to one newspaper, such as the *New York Times Index,* will serve as an index to all newspaper items of general interest, wherever published. This is not true, of course, in the case of strictly local-interest items.

New York Times Index. New York: New York Times, 1913– . (Semi-monthly; annual cumulation.) Gives exact reference to date, page, and column; serves as an index to articles of a general nature appearing in other newspapers.

LITERATURE IN COLLECTIONS

The practice of gathering extracts from the works of several writers into a collection is not a recent one. The name usually given to such a collection is "anthology," a word of Greek derivation which means flower-gathering and indicates that only the best pieces of literature are included.

The *Greek Anthology,* a collection of about 4,500 poems, inscriptions, and other kinds of writings by more than 300 writers, dates from ca. 60 B.C. The earliest English anthology dates from A.D. 975.

The original use of anthology to mean a volume containing only the "flower" of literature has been extended to mean any collection of extracts from the writings of various authors—often on one subject or of one kind, such as a collection of poems, short stories, essays, plays, speeches, or quotations.

Volumes of collected writings, including those called "readings," constitute an important part of any well-chosen library collection. Some of these collected works are analyzed in the card catalog (see pages 57–58). Most of them contain so many selections that it is not possible to include all of them in the card catalog.

INDEXES TO LITERATURE IN COLLECTIONS

The student will find that it is a tedious, and perhaps impossible, task to locate a particular essay, speech, or quotation, or a selection on a particular subject, by examining the index of every anthology. The reference

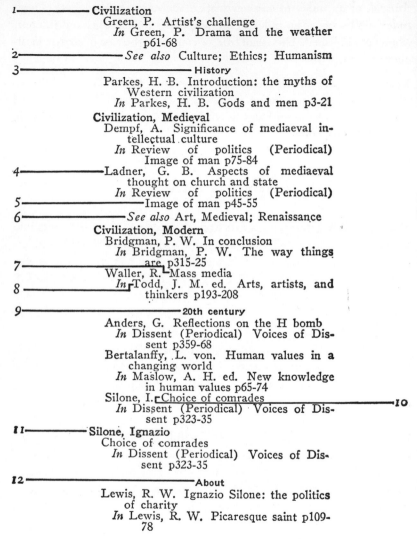

1———————**Civilization**
Green, P. Artist's challenge
In Green, P. Drama and the weather
p61-68
2———————*See also* Culture; Ethics; Humanism
3———————**History**
Parkes, H. B. Introduction: the myths of
Western civilization
In Parkes, H. B. Gods and men p3-21
Civilization, Medieval
Dempf, A. Significance of mediaeval in-
tellectual culture
In Review of politics (Periodical)
Image of man p75-84
4———————Ladner, G. B. Aspects of mediaeval
thought on church and state
In Review of politics (Periodical)
5———————Image of man p45-55
6———————*See also* Art, Medieval; Renaissance
Civilization, Modern
Bridgman, P. W. In conclusion
In Bridgman, P. W. The way things
7———————are p315-25
Waller, R. Mass media
8 ———————*In* Todd, J. M. ed. Arts, artists, and
thinkers p193-208
9———————**20th century**
Anders, G. Reflections on the H bomb
In Dissent (Periodical) Voices of Dissent p359-68
Bertalanffy, L. von. Human values in a
changing world
In Maslow, A. H. ed. New knowledge
in human values p65-74
Silone, I. Choice of comrades ————————*10*
In Dissent (Periodical) Voices of Dissent p323-35
11———————Silone, Ignazio
Choice of comrades
In Dissent (Periodical) Voices of Dissent p323-35
12———————**About**
Lewis, R. W. Ignazio Silone: the politics
of charity
In Lewis, R. W. Picaresque saint p109-
78

Figure 13   Excerpts from Essay and General Literature Index: *(1) subject heading; (2)* see also *references for the subject "Civilization"; (3) subheading under
"Civilization," i.e., Civilization—History; (4) author of essay "Aspects of Mediaeval
Thought on Church and State"; (5) title of the collection which includes the article
in 4; the author of* Image of Man *is the periodical* Review of Politics; *(6)* see also
*references for "Civilization, Medieval"; (7) title of an essay by R. Waller; (8)
editor of the collection entitled* Arts, Artists and Thinkers, *which includes the*

tool designed to facilitate this kind of search is the index to literature in collections.

Indexes to literature in collections follow the general pattern of the indexes to periodicals and newspapers, but they cover books only. There are indexes to general literature in collections, that is, essays, articles, and speeches covering a variety of subjects. An example of this kind of index is the *Essay and General Literature Index* (Figure 13). There are indexes to collections of poetry, stories, and plays. Examples are *Granger's Index to Poetry,* the *Short Story Index,* and the *Play Index.* Indexing is by author, subject, and title, and the location reference includes the name of the compiler of the anthology, the title of the anthology, and the page or pages on which the essay, poem, story, or play can be found.

Indexes to poetry, short stories, and plays are discussed in Chapter Twenty-two, Literature. Examples of indexes to collections of literature which cover several subject areas are listed below.

Biography Index. New York: The H. W. Wilson Company, 1946– . Indexes current books of individual and collective biography.

Essay and General Literature Index. New York: The H. W. Wilson Company, 1934– . Indexes collections of essays, articles, and speeches relating to the several subject fields.

Granger's Index to Poetry and Recitations. 3d ed. revised and enlarged. Chicago: A. C. McClurg & Company, 1940. Indexes by title, author, and first line collections of poetry, recitations in poetry and prose, dialogues, orations, and selections from drama.

---

essay in 7; (9) subheading of "Civilization, Modern," i.e., Civilization, Modern —Twentieth century; (10) title of an article by I. Silone in a collection of articles from the periodical, Dissent, *entitled* Voices of Dissent; *the periodical is the author of the collection; (11) full name of the author of the article "Choice of Comrades" in 10; (12) indicates that the article which follows is about Ignazio Silone, not by him.* (Essay and General Literature Index. *New York: The H. W. Wilson Company, June, 1959, pp. 30 and 139.*)

❧ CHAPTER TEN ❧

BIOGRAPHICAL DICTIONARIES

BIOGRAPHY, from the two Greek words *bios,* meaning life, and *graphein,* meaning to write, is that form of history which is applied to individuals rather than to nations or civilizations. It is the purpose of biography to tell accurately the history of an individual from his birth to his death in a manner that will reveal the various aspects of his character, personality, and philosophy.

Since ancient times, men have been interested in the lives of other men, either from a desire to eulogize them, to learn from them, or to imitate them, or just from simple curiosity.

Toward the end of the first century A.D., Plutarch wrote his *Parallel Lives,* the life histories of forty-six Greeks and Romans. The word "biography," however, did not appear in the English language until 1683, when John Dryden described this work of Plutarch's as the "history of particular men's lives." This meaning of biography, as the history of the life of an individual, has become established as a literary form.

Other literary forms contribute to biography but must be distinguished from it. They are:

1 Autobiography, the narration of a person's life by himself
2 Memoirs, the history of his times as seen by the individual who writes them
3 Diary, a day-by-day account of the happenings and events in a person's life, recorded by that person
4 Letters, written communications of a personal nature (as distinguished from *belles-lettres,* meaning literature), which may be intimate narratives, records of events, or expressions of the writer's thoughts and philosophy.

Biography may draw from these and other sources to present all of the significant characteristics of the subject.

The outstanding example of individual biography in English—or in any language—is James Boswell's *Life of Samuel Johnson,* written in the eighteenth century. Since that time biography has become an increasingly important form of literature and occupies a prominent place in all library collections. The student who seeks material on a country, a civilization, or a period of history will do well to include in his search an investigation of the lives of outstanding persons who were a part of that country, civilization, or period of history, even though individual biographies are not considered reference books.

Biography as a literary form differs in purpose, style, and content from simple biographical information about an individual.

In the nineteenth century, there appeared in most European countries publications called "dictionaries of national biography," presenting biographical information about all important national figures. These collections of biographical articles were the forerunners of the modern biographical dictionary, a work which combines biography (factual information about the life of an individual) and dictionary (alphabetical arrangement).

The biographical dictionary, with biographical sketches arranged alphabetically by surname, does not qualify as true biography, since it does not present all aspects of an individual's life. However, the *Dictionary of National Biography* and the *Dictionary of American Biography* are outstanding for their scholarly and objective treatment of the persons included.

Biographical dictionaries are among the most frequently used books in the college library (or in any library). Questions about notable people and about people in the news—their lives, interests, education, background, affiliations, position, and even their addresses—come from faculty and students alike.

There are numerous sources of biographical information concerning individuals; these include encyclopedias, encyclopedia annuals, and dictionaries. However, the reference books which were written for the specific purpose of quickly and conveniently providing the kinds of biographical information mentioned above are:

1   Biographical indexes, which point out books, periodicals, and other sources (excluding biographical dictionaries) in which the information can be found
2   Biographical dictionaries, which contain the information sought

KINDS OF BIOGRAPHICAL DICTIONARIES

Biographical dictionaries can be divided into three classes according to the nationality, the profession, and the dates of the persons included:

1   Universal—not limited to any state, country, or profession
    a   Persons no longer living
    b   Living persons
2   National or regional—limited in coverage to particular countries or regions but including persons from all of the professions and occupations
    a   Persons no longer living
    b   Living persons
3   Professional or occupational—limited to persons in a specific profession or occupation
    a   Universal
        (1)   Persons no longer living
        (2)   Living persons

   b National or regional
     (1) Persons no longer living
     (2) Living persons

CHOOSING A BIOGRAPHICAL DICTIONARY

It is necessary to learn which biographical dictionaries belong in each class and to learn the outstanding characteristics of each one in order to use them with any degree of efficiency.

To determine which biographical dictionary will provide information on a particular person, it is necessary to establish, if possible, the following facts about that person:

1 His dates of birth and death, if he is not living
2 His nationality
3 His profession or occupation

Sources which will aid in establishing these facts are:

1 The card catalog. If the individual has written a book, and if this book is listed in the card catalog, the dates of his birth and death will be given immediately following his name on the catalog card. The subject matter of the book or books by him and about him may indicate his field of work, and the place of publication may provide a clue to his nationality.

2 The *Cumulative Book Index.* If the card catalog does not include any books by or about the person in question, the *Cumulative Book Index,* which is a world list of books in the English language, will list the books he has written in English, together with his dates.

3 *The Biography Index.* This index to biographical articles appearing in books and magazines (excluding biographical dictionaries) gives the dates and the profession of all persons it includes. If the individual is not an American, his nationality is given also.

4 Periodical indexes. Any periodical articles by or about the person on whom the student seeks information will be listed in one of the indexes to periodical literature. The periodicals in which the articles appear often include a brief statement about the author. The dates

of publication of these articles may provide a clue to the time when the individual might have been included in a biographical dictionary or was in the current news. The subject matter of the articles will indicate his field of interest, and the place of publication may suggest his nationality. Indexes to periodical literature also list obituaries, which often provide full biographical information.

5 A book by the person in question. The title page may list the author's position, such as Professor of History at McGill University, or Professor of English, Duke University, immediately following his name. The location of the university may be a clue to the nationality of the person who teaches there. The position he holds indicates his profession.

The advantage gained by making an effort to establish the dates, the nationality, and the profession of a person before looking for him in any biographical dictionary will more than make up for the time spent in locating this information. For example, if the subject is an important contemporary American statesman, the following biographical dictionaries will be eliminated from consideration immediately:

Who's Who
Dictionary of American Biography
Dictionary of National Biography
Appleton's Cyclopaedia of American Biography

Among the biographical dictionaries which are possible sources of information about a living American statesman are:

Who's Who in America
Current Biography
International Who's Who
Century Dictionary of Names

It is necessary to point out that in some cases none of the above-mentioned sources—card catalog, periodical indexes, *Cumulative Book Index, Biography Index,* or books by the individual—will provide his dates, nationality, or profession. In such cases, locating biographical material about the individual becomes a tedious process of trial and error. Even when dates, nationality, and profession have been established, it is not always possible to find the subject in the biographical dictionary or dictionaries designed to cover his profession, his nationality, and his time of prominence. Biographical information in the several biographical dictionaries is provided, for the most part, at the request of the publisher by the individuals included. The fact that a person is not included may mean that he failed to furnish the biographical information requested and that the publisher was unable to secure it from other sources. In these cases, it may be necessary to identify the individual by piecing together bits of information from the book jacket of one of his books, from a few titles of periodical articles by or about him, and from the fact that he is editor of, or contributes to, one of the professional journals.

USING A BIOGRAPHICAL DICTIONARY

Before using any biographical dictionary the first time, it is important to read the preliminary pages to determine (1) whether the alphabetical arrangement is letter-by-letter or word-by-word; (2) what special features are included; and (3) what abbreviations and symbols are used. The method of selecting names to be included should be noted, as a test of the objectivity of the work.

REPRESENTATIVE BIOGRAPHICAL DICTIONARIES

Universal Biography

PERSONS NO LONGER LIVING

New Century Cyclopedia of Names. New York: Appleton-Century-Crofts, Inc., 1954. 3 vols. Identifies proper names of importance today: persons, places, events, literary characters, plays, operas, mythological and legendary names; provides a chronological table of world history.

Thomas, Joseph. *Universal Pronouncing Dictionary of Biography and Mythology.* 5th ed. Philadelphia: J. P. Lippincott Company, 1930. Gives biographical sketches of notable persons; includes mythological characters; has some bibliography.

Webster's Biographical Dictionary. Springfield, Mass.: G. & C. Merriam Company, 1943. Gives brief, concise biographical sketches; includes pronunciation.

LIVING PERSONS

Current Biography: Who's News and Why. New York: The H. W. Wilson Company, 1940– . (Monthly, except August.) Presents up-to-the-minute information on names in the news, with photographs of the biographees; includes bibliography; provides in each issue a cumulated index to previous issues.

International Who's Who. London: Europa Publications, Ltd., 1935– . (Annual.) Includes sketches of important people in the world today.

The New Century Cyclopedia of Names.

Webster's Biographical Dictionary.

World Biography. 5th ed. Bethpage, N.Y.: Institute for Research in Biography, Inc., 1954. (1st ed., 1940.) An international encyclopedia of contemporary biography; includes notable persons in all professions.

National or Regional Biography

PERSONS NO LONGER LIVING

Appleton's Cyclopaedia of American Biography. Rev. ed. New York: D. Appleton and Company, Inc., 1887–1900. 7 vols. Includes all important persons identified with American history from its earliest beginnings.

Dictionary of American Biography. Published under the auspices of the American Council of Learned Societies. New York: Charles Scribner's Sons, 1928–1944. 21 vols. *Supplement* 2. To December 31, 1940. New York: Charles Scribner's Sons, 1958. (First supplement is Vol 21.) A scholarly work; provides lengthy signed articles and bibliography.

Dictionary of National Biography. Edited by Leslie Stephen and Sidney Lee. London: Oxford University Press, 1922. 22 vols. *Supplements*, 1901–1911, 1912–1921, 1922–1930, 1931–1940, 1941–1950. Provides full, accurate biographies of all notable inhabitants of Great Britain and the colonies (exclusive of living persons) from the earliest historical period to the present time; includes bibliography.

National Cyclopaedia of American Biography. New York: James T. White & Company, 1888– . 52 vols. to date. (Vol. 53 in progress.) Ranks with the national biographical dictionaries of Europe; presents a complete political, social, commercial, and industrial history of the United States; not alphabetically arranged, but has a detailed index.

Who Was Who. London: A. & C. Black, Ltd., 1929–1952. 4 vols. Companion to *Who's Who;* contains biographies of persons in *Who's Who* who have died, with the date of death added.

Who Was Who in America. Chicago: Marquis–Who's Who, Inc., 1942–1960. 3 vols. Gives biographies of persons in *Who's Who in America* who have died, with date of death added.

LIVING PERSONS

National Cyclopaedia of American Biography. Includes living persons in the current volumes.

Who's Who. London: A. & C. Black, Ltd., 1849– . (Annual.) The first "who's who"; includes persons of distinction in all fields; covers Great Britain and the Commonwealth nations.

Who's Who in America. Chicago: Marquis–Who's Who, Inc., 1899– . (Biennial.) Includes persons of special prominence in every line of work and those who are selected arbitrarily because of their position in government, religion, education, industry, and other fields.

Other useful biographies of the "who's who" type, which include eminent living persons from all professions, are:

American Catholic Who's Who
Who's Who in France
Who's Who in Germany
Who's Who in Israel
Who's Who of American Women

In addition to those listed above, there are biographical dictionaries by race, by section of a country, and by profession.

Professional and occupational biographical dictionaries are discussed in the chapters which treat each subject field.

INDEXES TO BIOGRAPHY

In addition to the biographical dictionaries which provide needed information, there are indexes which point out biographies in books and in periodical literature. The following indexes indicate where biographical material can be found and give the titles and pages of books or the volumes, dates, and pages of periodicals.

Biography Index. New York: The H. W. Wilson Company, 1946– . (Quarterly; annual cumulations which are replaced by three-year permanent volumes.) Locates biographical material of all types in current books in the English language and in periodicals; gives dates of birth and death, profession, and nationality, if other than American.

Essay and General Literature Index. New York: The H. W. Wilson Company, 1934– . Indexes biography found in collected works.

Hefling, Helen, and Dyde, Jessie. *Hefling and Richards' Index to Contemporary Biography and Criticism*. 2d ed. Boston: F. W. Faxon Company, 1934. Includes persons born 1850 or later; covers many fields; gives dates.

CHAPTER ELEVEN

ATLASES AND GAZETTEERS

BEFORE he could write, and perhaps before he could speak, primitive man left landmarks (cairns) to show where he had been. The oldest known map is a Babylonian clay tablet dating from about 2300 B.C. There are many other clay tablets which show geographical locations.

The Greeks, using their knowledge of science, philosophy, mathematics, geography, and astronomy, succeeded in developing map making (cartography) to a point not again attained until the sixteenth century. Greek geographers from the fifth century B.C. believed that the earth is a sphere. About A.D. 150, Claudius Ptolemy of Alexandria, perhaps the greatest single contributor in history to cartography and geography, compiled his eight-volume *Geographia,* the first scientific and comprehensive treatment of cartography. It contained, in addition to the text, twenty-eight maps and a list of all of the principal places then known. The *Geographia* disappeared during the Middle Ages and was not found until the fifteenth century. Its rediscovery[1] helped make possible the

[1] The *Geographia* had been preserved by the Arabs.

voyages of Columbus, Magellan, Vasco da Gama, John Cabot, and others, thus hastening the era of discovery and exploration. In turn, the discoveries of these explorers greatly increased the demand for maps.

The importance of the invention of printing in this period of discovery and exploration cannot be overemphasized. Hundreds of maps could now be made from the same plates at low cost, and hundreds of persons could own them. The earliest printed maps were woodcuts; these were followed by copper engravings.

Important contributors to map making during this period were Mercator, famous for his celestial and terrestrial globes and for his system of projection, and Ortelius, credited with the publication of the first modern atlas in 1570. Both were members of the Dutch school of cartography.

ATLASES

A map is a representation, usually flat, of the earth's surface or a part of it or of the celestial sphere or a part of it.[2] An atlas is a collection of maps, usually bound together in one volume. The word "atlas" was first used in this sense by Mercator from the figure of the mythological Atlas, which was often used as the frontispiece of early collections of maps. It has come to mean any volume containing not only maps, but also plates, engravings, charts, and tables, with or without descriptive text. It is sometimes used as the name of a volume in which subjects are presented in tabular form

While it is generally recognized that atlases are essential in studying history,[3] geography, and other branches of the social sciences, it is becoming increasingly apparent that many atlases are valuable also as general reference books because of the descriptive materials they contain in addition to maps. Today, as the world becomes "smaller," maps can be considered necessary companions to the daily newspaper and radio

---

[2] *Webster's New Collegiate Dictionary* (Springfield, Mass.: G. & C. Merriam Company, 1960), p. 513.

[3] A historical atlas is a collection of modern maps (not a collection of old maps) which delineates past events or periods of history.

and television news commentary, verifying names, places, and events in the news and presenting them in proper geographical relationship to other names, places, and events.

There are many sources of maps. Most of the general encyclopedias include maps either in a separate volume or as illustrative material within the text; encyclopedia annuals include up-to-date maps; many handbooks, almanacs, newspapers, and periodicals also contain maps. However, the atlas is the reference book designed primarily to provide maps of all kinds.

Atlases vary in quality, and they vary according to the country of publication. For example, an atlas of the world which is published in America will include more or larger maps of America than one published in France. The latter will include larger maps of France.

CHOOSING AN ATLAS

To be able to choose an atlas to answer a given question, it is necessary to know certain things about each atlas.

1   The scope
    a   Is it world-wide in coverage, or is it limited to one or more regions?
    b   Does it include all kinds of maps, or only maps of a specific nature?
    c   Does it provide descriptive material about the various geographical locations?
2   The place of publication as an indication of emphasis
3   The date of publication as an indication of its up-to-dateness
4   The kind of index
    a   Is there one comprehensive index for the entire volume, or are there separate indexes for each map or section of maps?
    b   Is the index a separate volume, or is it a part of the atlas?
    c   Does it indicate pronunciation?
    d   Is the reference to the location on a given map clear and definite?
5   The quality and content of the maps
    a   Is the scale indicated clearly?
    b   Are the symbols distinct and easily read?
    c   Are the projections in keeping with the purpose of the map?

d   Is the lettering clear and legible?
e   Is the coloring varied and well differentiated?
f   Is the legend clearly explained?
g   Are the names of countries given in the language of each country
    or in translation?

GAZETTEERS

A gazetteer is a dictionary of geographical places. In addition to geo-graphic location, it gives historical, statistical, cultural, and other relevant information about these places. It may also indicate pronunciation. Because they provide a variety of factual material about places, gazetteers are important reference sources. Recent editions describe a place as it is now; old editions give historical information about it. The economic growth or decline of a town or city, as indicated by data on population, number of industries, schools, and so on, will often be shown by the brief facts given in gazetteers over a period of years.

In using a gazetteer, it is important to note the copyright date as an indication of the recency of the material; the system of pronunciation and the abbreviations used; the arrangement of the material; and any additional material, such as maps and tables, which may be included in appendices.

USEFUL ATLASES AND GAZETTEERS

Bartholomew, John W. (ed.). *Advanced Atlas of Modern Geography*. 3d ed. New York: McGraw-Hill Book Company, Inc., 1957. Covers the world by regions, with emphasis on the physiographic features of each area; includes world and continental maps, geographical terms.

———. *The Times Atlas of the World*. Vol. I: *The World, Australasia & East Asia*. Vol. II: *South-west Asia & Russia*. Vol. III: *Northern Europe*. Vol. IV: *Southern Europe and Africa*. Vol. V: *The Americas*. Mid-century edition. London: The Times Publishing Company, Ltd., 1955–1959. Each volume includes an index-gazetteer.

Collocott, T. C., and Thorne, J. O. (eds.). *Macmillan World Gazetteer and Geographical Dictionary*. Revised ed. New York: The Macmillan Company, 1957. Provides brief geographical and historical information about places throughout the world.

Encyclopaedia Britannica World Atlas. Chicago: Encyclopaedia Britannica, Inc., 1960. Presents political and physical maps, geographical summaries and comparisons, and a glossary of geographical terms.

Espenshade, Edward B. (ed.). *Goode's World Atlas*. 11th ed. Chicago: Rand McNally & Company, 1960. Gives—in maps—the physical, political, and economic features of the world; has a pronouncing index. Formerly *Goode's School Atlas*.

Hammond's Ambassador World Atlas. Maplewood, N.J.: C. S. Hammond & Co., Inc., 1954. Contains political and physical maps, including those which show rainfall, vegetation, population; provides useful gazetteer information about some places and maps of some of the large cities.

Rand McNally Standard World Atlas. Chicago: Rand McNally & Company, 1958. Presents selected world information and comparisons in maps; includes climatic tables and a chart of world political information showing area, population, government, capital, largest city.

Seltzer, Leon E. (ed.). *Columbia-Lippincott Gazetteer of the World*. New York: Columbia University Press, 1952. Includes facts about population, trade, industry, agricultural and natural resources, and cultural institutions.

Webster's Geographical Dictionary. Revised ed. Springfield, Mass.: G. & C. Merriam Company, 1959. Provides geographical and historical information about places; gives pronunciation.

CHAPTER TWELVE

YEARBOOKS AND HANDBOOKS

EVERY library has a number of books for quick reference which provide brief information on a multitude of subjects. Among these "ready-reference" works are yearbooks and handbooks.

A yearbook is a publication which is issued annually for the purpose of giving current information in narrative, statistical, or directory form. There are several types of yearbooks:

1 Encyclopedia annuals, issued by the major encyclopedia publishers as a means of keeping the encyclopedia up-to-date, are comprehensive in coverage and give a summary of all the major events of the preceding year.

2 Almanacs, which were originally calendars of months and days with special dates and anniversaries, forecasts of the weather, and astronomical calculations, are now collections of miscellaneous facts and statistics.

3 Directories, which list persons or organizations in alphabetical or

classified arrangement, include addresses and affiliations for individuals and officers and other data for organizations.

A handbook (literally a small book which can be held in the hand) is a volume which treats broad subjects in brief fashion. It may include odd bits of information about a variety of topics. Among the most useful handbooks are:

1 Manuals, which give instruction on, or serve as guides to, occupations, hobbies, art forms, trades, etc.
2 Miscellanies, which include bits of unusual and hard-to-find information on many subjects
3 Compendiums, which provide brief but comprehensive summaries of a subject[1]
4 Companions, which explain and interpret various aspects of a subject[1]
5 Digests, which present in condensed form information that is classified and arranged under proper headings or titles; examples are digests of laws, digests of articles from periodicals, or digests of the plots of novels, short stories, dramas, or poems

SELECTION AND USE OF A YEARBOOK OR HANDBOOK

Each yearbook and handbook is designed to provide certain kinds of information for the purpose of answering specific kinds of questions. Therefore, before attempting to choose a yearbook or a handbook, the student must examine his question.

1 Does it require statistical information?
2 Is it a directory-type question?
3 Is it a "trend" question?
4 Does it come under the heading of miscellany?

In order to use a yearbook or a handbook quickly and satisfactorily, it is necessary to understand:

[1] Compendiums and companions are explained in greater detail in the chapter on literature.

1 The organization and arrangement of material
   a Is it organized into chapters or into broad general subjects, and does it have a detailed table of contents and/or a comprehensive index?
   b Is it broken down into small topics, arranged alphabetically?
   c Does it have tables only, or does it give both text and tables?
2 The kinds of material included
   a Is it statistical? If it is, does it give the source for the statistics presented?
   b Does it give instructions and directions?
   c Is it a collection of miscellaneous information?
3 The scope
   a Does it cover all countries and all subjects?
   b Is it limited to one country and to a selected number of subjects?
4 The period covered
   a Is it one year? Two years?
   b If it is a handbook, is it revised often?
5 Special aids to the reader
   a Does it provide bibliographical references for further reading?
   b Does it provide cross references?
   c Is the illustrative material—charts, tables, maps, pictures—appropriate and adequate?
6 The kinds of questions it will answer
   a Will it answer factual and statistical questions?
   b Will it provide "trend" and background information?

REPRESENTATIVE YEARBOOKS AND HANDBOOKS

Yearbooks

ENCYCLOPEDIA ANNUALS

Americana Annual. New York: Americana Corporation, 1923– . Covers events of the previous year; features a brief chronological listing of events.

Britannica Book of the Year. Chicago: Encyclopaedia Britannica, Inc., 1938– . Gives a calendar of events, many short articles under specific titles, statistics, and bibliography.

Collier's Year Book. New York: P. F. Collier & Son Corporation, 1938– .
   Surveys the events of the year; is especially strong in sports and
   chronology; has a supplementary almanac.

The World Book Encyclopedia Annual Supplement. Chicago: Field Enterprises, 1922– . Reviews events and developments of the year with
   emphasis on articles of interest to young people.

ALMANACS

Information Please Almanac. Edited by John Kieran. Supervised by Dan
   Golenpaul Associates. New York: Publisher varies, 1947– . Includes
   miscellaneous information arranged in general classes; has an alphabetically arranged subject index.

The World Almanac and Book of Facts. New York: The World Telegram
   and Sun, 1868– . Gives comprehensive coverage of factual material
   of all kinds; index is in the front of the book.

COMPENDIUMS

American Yearbook. New York: Publisher varies, 1929– . Covers all
   countries, but emphasizes the United States; has long articles which
   include bibliography.

The Statesman's Yearbook. London: Macmillan & Co., Ltd., 1864– .
   Covers government, area, population, education, religion, social welfare,
   money, industry, and other statistical and historical information about
   the countries of the world.

U.S. Bureau of the Census. *Statistical Abstract of the United States.* Washington, D.C.: Government Printing Office, 1878– . Summarizes
   statistics of political, industrial, economic, and social institutions and
   organizations in the United States; provides bibliography.

Handbooks

Chambers, Robert (ed.). *The Book of Days.* Edinburgh: W. & R. Chambers,
   Ltd., 1899. Arranged by the day of the year; gives many oddities and
   curiosities; places emphasis on the United Kingdom.

Douglas, George William (ed.). *The American Book of Days.* 2d ed. Revised
   by Helen Douglas Compton. New York: The H. W. Wilson Company,
   1948. Provides the history, origin, and customary observance of holidays
   and festivals, notably American, Christian, and Jewish.

Kane, Joseph Nathan. *Famous First Facts.* Revised and enlarged ed. New
   York: The H. W. Wilson Company, 1950. Includes all information in

the earlier edition and in *More First Facts,* with new material about events, discoveries, and inventions in the United States.

Post, Emily. *Etiquette.* 10th ed. New York: Funk & Wagnalls Company, 1960. Treats social usage.

Shankle, George E. *American Nicknames.* 2d ed. New York: The H. W. Wilson Company, 1955. Gives origin and significance of nicknames applied to American celebrities of the past and present and to states, cities, towns, athletic teams, and the like.

❧ CHAPTER THIRTEEN ❧

BIBLIOGRAPHIES

THE word "bibliography," deriving from two Greek words, *biblion* meaning book and *graphein* meaning to write, was used in post-classical Greece in the sense of the writing of books. The scribes who copied books were the first bibliographers. This meaning was in use as late as 1761, as is indicated by the definition of the word "bibliographer" in Fenning's *English Dictionary* of that date as "one who copies books."

The transition from the meaning of writing *of* books to that of writing *about* books came about in France in the eighteenth century; the latter meaning is in use today.

In the sense of writing about books, the term bibliography has several uses:

1   It is the systematic description of groups of books, manuscripts, and other publications as to authorship, title, edition, and imprint, and their enumeration and arrangement into lists for purposes of information.[1]

1 See Chapter Twenty-three, pp. 206–209.

2   It is the name given to a list of books, manuscripts, and other publica-
    tions, systematically described and arranged, which have some rela-
    tionship to each other. Thus, there are several kinds of bibliographies.

    a   General—not limited to one author, subject, country, or period
    of time

    b   Author—listing the works by and about one author

    c   Subject—restricted to one subject or to one subject field

    d   National or regional—including material relating to one country
    or to one region

    e   Trade—directed to the book trade and supplying information
    needed in buying and selling books

3   It is the science of books, that branch of learning concerned with the
    historical and technical examination of written works, in which books
    and manuscripts are examined to discover or verify their origin, dates,
    number and order of pages, authorship, and textual material.

A bibliography may be complete, including *all* works of a particular
kind, or it may be selective, containing only a part of the works. It may
be descriptive, having only a brief descriptive note (annotation); it may
be evaluative, that is, with critical comment; or it may be both descriptive
and evaluative.

Bibliographies may be found in individual books, in periodical
articles, and in encyclopedias and other reference books. In addition to
this type of bibliography, compiled for a specific book or article, there
are bibliographies, both of a general nature and in the subject fields,
which are designed as *reference books,* to aid the researcher in his quest
for material. Whether they are lists of further readings, enumerations of
the sources used in writing the book or the article, or bibliographies of the
reference-book type, bibliographies are useful sources in any search for
material on a subject.

1   They locate material on the subject in question.

2   They provide a means of verifying such items as author's name, com-
    plete title of work, place of publication, publisher, date of publication,
    edition, and number of pages.

3   If they are annotated, they indicate the scope of the subject and the
    manner in which it is treated; if the annotation is critical and evalua-
    tive, it comments upon the usefulness of the publication.

4 They point out material, including parts of books, which cannot be analyzed in the card catalog.
5 They group works according to form, location, and period.

Bibliographies in the subject fields are discussed in Chapters Sixteen to Twenty-two.

REPRESENTATIVE BIBLIOGRAPHIES OF THE REFERENCE-BOOK TYPE

General Bibliographies

Besterman, Theodore. *A World Bibliography of Bibliographies*. 3d and final ed. New York: Scarecrow Press, 1955–1956. 4 vols. International in scope; includes bibliographical catalogs, calendars, abstracts, and digests.

The Bibliographic Index. New York: The H. W. Wilson Company, 1938– . (Semiannual; annual and larger cumulations.) A subject index to current bibliographies; includes those published as books and pamphlets and those which appear in books, pamphlets, and periodical articles, both in English and in foreign languages.

Bibliographies of Periodical Publications

N. W. Ayer & Son's Directory of Newspapers and Periodicals. Philadelphia: N. W. Ayer & Son, Inc., 1880– . Provides information about newspapers and periodicals printed in the United States and its possessions, Canada, Bermuda, Panama, and the Philippines; includes information about the towns and cities in which they are published.

Ulrich's Periodicals Directory. 9th ed. New York: R. R. Bowker Company, 1959. Lists titles by subject class, with detailed index and cross references; includes foreign periodicals.

Selective and Evaluative Bibliographies

Booklist. Chicago: The American Library Association, 1905– . (Semi-monthly; monthly in August.) A highly selective list of currently published books designed to meet the needs of the average public library; is arranged by Dewey Decimal Classification, fiction, books for children, books for young people, U.S. government publications, pamphlets, etc.

Hoffman, Hester R. (ed.). *The Reader's Adviser and Bookman's Manual.* 9th ed. revised and enlarged. New York: R. R. Bowker Company, 1960. A guide to the best in print in literature, biographies, dictionaries, encyclopedias, bibles, classics, drama, poetry, fiction, science, philosophy, travel, history (subtitle).

"The Standard Catalog Series." New York: The H. W. Wilson Company. Includes *Children's Catalog, Standard Catalog for High School Libraries,* and *Standard Catalog for Public Libraries;* provides annotated lists of books for the type of library covered.

Subscription Books Bulletin. Chicago: American Library Association, 1930– 1956. Combined with *Booklist* in September, 1956; gives unbiased, critical reviews of reference books; indicates whether or not the work is recommended.

Winchell, Constance M. *Guide to Reference Books.* 7th ed. Based on *Guide to Reference Books,* 6th ed., by Isadore Gilbert Mudge. Chicago: American Library Association, 1951. (*Supplements,* 1950–1952, 1953–1955, and 1956–1958.) An evaluative list of selected reference books; indicates the comparative value of books.

Trade Bibliographies

American Book Publishing Record. New York: R. R. Bowker Company, 1960– . (Monthly.) Presents a complete record of American book publication in the four (sometimes five) calendar weeks preceding its date of issue; is a subject index to *Publishers' Weekly.*

Books in Print. New York: R. R. Bowker Company, 1948– . (Annual.) Indexes the *Publishers' Trade List Annual* by author, title, and series; gives publisher and price of book; covers *only* the publishers included in *Publishers' Trade List Annual.*

Cumulative Book Index. New York: The H. W. Wilson Company, 1898– . (Frequently cumulated monthly issues; bound semiannual and larger cumulations.) "A world list of books in the English language"; lists all books included by author, subject, editor, translator; has many title, series, and illustrator entries; gives author, title, price, publisher, date of publication for each entry; supplements the *U.S. Catalog.*

Publishers' Weekly. New York: Publishers' Weekly, 1872– . The American book-trade journal; contains lists of new publications of the week and books announced for publication, news items, and editorials.

Publishers Trade List Annual. New York: Publishers' Weekly, 1873– .

An annual compilation of publishers' catalogs; provides a list of most of the books currently in print in America; not all publishers are included.

Subject Guide to Books in Print. New York: R. R. Bowker, 1957– . (Annual.) A subject index to *Publishers' Trade List Annual;* indexes according to the subject headings established by the Library of Congress.

U.S. Catalog. 4th ed. New York: The H. W. Wilson Company, 1928. Lists books in English in print on January 1, 1928, by author, title, and subject; gives author, title, edition, publisher, price, and generally, date, paging, and illustrations; continued currently by *Cumulative Book Index*.

CHAPTER FOURTEEN

SPECIAL MATERIALS

IN addition to books, magazines, and newspapers, which have been discussed in the preceding chapters, the library provides a number of special kinds of source materials for the student who is seeking the answer to a question, aid in solving or clarifying a problem, or illustrative material in any of the several subject fields. Since these materials are not always listed in the general catalog, it is important that users of the library know what they are, how they are organized and arranged, and the rules which govern their use.

Among these special materials are (1) pamphlets and clippings; (2) audio-visual aids; (3) microfilms, microcards, and microprint; and (4) government publications.

PAMPHLETS AND CLIPPINGS

A pamphlet is a publication which deals with only one subject and consists of a few pages stitched together and inclosed in paper covers. Pamphlets may be issued singly or in a series such as the "Headline Books" of the Foreign Policy Association. Pamphlets cover topics of current importance in any subject field and appear more frequently in areas of thought and activity which are constantly changing.

When they are first published, pamphlets are excellent sources of recent information or opinion on a subject. Parts of books may appear first as pamphlets, and writings which have never been published in book form are often found in pamphlet form.

When pamphlets become out-of-date as current information, they serve as valuable historical sources because they indicate the trend of interest and opinion at a particular time.

Pamphlets are organized for use in several ways:

1 Some are classified, cataloged, and shelved in the general collection.
2 Some are listed in the card catalog but arranged in a filing cabinet.
3 Others may be filed in a cabinet designated as the Pamphlet File, arranged alphabetically by subject or numerically if part of a series. In this case, there is usually a separate catalog or listing of the available pamphlets on or near the filing cabinet.

Clippings which have been taken from newspapers, magazines, brochures, and other sources are useful for current events and for providing information on subjects too brief to be treated in pamphlets or books.

Clippings may be mounted on cardboard or placed in folders. In general, they are kept in a vertical file and are arranged alphabetically by subject. As a rule, they are not listed in the main catalog.

AUDIO-VISUAL AIDS

Included in the broad field of audio-visual aids are pictures (clipped from newspapers and magazines), postcards, reproductions of art masterpieces, slides, filmstrips, motion-picture films, charts, graphs, maps, models, phonograph records, tape and wire recordings, and sheet music.

These materials are useful in art and music appreciation courses, in the study of drama and literature, in learning languages, as illustrative aids for class assignments, and for recreational and cultural purposes.

Audio-visual materials may be listed in the general catalog, or they may be kept in separate files in a special room, with a catalog or listing for each kind of material. Thus a library may have a map file, a picture file, a darkroom where films, slides, and filmstrips are kept and projected, and a listening room for phonograph records and tape recordings.

Regulations governing the use of these materials vary greatly. In some libraries, certain kinds of materials are circulated while others must be used in the library. In other libraries, all materials must be used in the library.

MICROFILMS, MICROCARDS, AND MICROPRINT

A microfilm is a greatly reduced photographic reproduction of printed matter on film of standard motion-picture size or smaller. It was developed as a means of saving space by microcopying back issues of newspapers and magazines, but it is used also to reproduce parts of books needed for research.

A microcard is a microscopic photographic reproduction of printed material on standard-size library catalog cards. A microcard contains up to eighty pages of printed material. Entire books are now produced in microcard form.

Microprint is a microphotograph reproduced in printed form. Microfilm might be compared to the negative of a picture taken by a camera, microcard and microprint to the final snapshot. All forms of microphotography must be read with the aid of a reading machine. Microfilm, microcards, and microprint are thought of, first of all, as aids in advanced research, but in the library which keeps its back issues of magazines and newspapers in some microphotographic form, the undergraduate student must learn how to consult these materials when he is looking for pertinent data on a subject.

Microfilm and microprint may be cataloged and shelved with the main collection, but the usual practice is to catalog and shelve them in a separate place. Microcards may be filed in the library's main catalog; in most cases, however, they are kept in a separate file.

REFERENCE BOOKS ON SPECIAL MATERIALS

Ballou, Hubbard Walter (comp.). *Guide to Microreproduction Equipment.* Annapolis, Md.: National Microfilm Association, 1959. Includes descriptive information on equipment and films.

De Kieffer, Robert, and Cochran, Lee W. *Manual of Audio-Visual Techniques.* Englewood Cliffs, N.J.: Prentice-Hall, Inc., 1955. Provides brief information about many kinds of audio-visual materials and explains the correct techniques for handling them; includes a bibliography for each section.

Educational Film Guide. New York: The H. W. Wilson Company, 1936– . (Annual supplements.) Lists and describes 16mm educational films; includes an alphabetical listing by title and subject and a directory of sources.

Educators Guide to Free Science Materials. Randolph, Wis.: Educators Progress Service, 1960– . (Annual.) Presents an annotated list of free films, filmstrips, bulletins, pamphlets, charts, and like materials, giving information on the nature, purposes, and uses of these materials.

Educators Guide to Free Tapes, Scripts, Transcriptions. Randolph, Wis.: Educators Progress Service, 1955– . Describes and gives pertinent information about the nature, purposes, and uses of these materials.

Filmstrip Guide. New York: The H. W. Wilson Company, 1948– . (Annual supplements.) Lists by title and subject; describes current filmstrips for sale or free loan.

Hastings, Henry C. (comp.). *Spoken Poetry on Records and Tapes.* Chicago: Association of College and Reference Libraries, 1957. An index of currently available recordings (subtitle).

McClusky, Frederick Dean (comp.). *A-V Bibliography.* 2d. ed. Dubuque, Iowa: W. C. Brown Company, 1955. Provides a comprehensive bibliography of the literature on audio-visual instruction.

Public Affairs Information Service Bulletin. New York: Public Affairs Information Service, 1915– . (Weekly.) Indexes books, documents, pamphlets, periodical literature, reports of private and public agencies, government publications relating to economic and social conditions, public administration, and international relations; a selective subject list.

Vertical File Service Catalog. New York: The H. W. Wilson Company, 1932– . (Monthly.) Lists and describes current pamphlets, booklets, and leaflets.

A government publication is a publication issued (or purchased) at public expense by authority of Congress or any other government office or institution—national, state, or local—for distribution to government officials or to the public.

Government publications grow out of the peculiar function of the governmental agencies which issue them and are a public record of the operation and activities of government. They provide a means of keeping the public informed, so that each citizen can understand and make use of the services the government provides and can carry out more intelligently his duties as a citizen.

The documents containing the records of government in their original form, that is, before they are published, are placed in government archives. In published form, they are made available to libraries, organizations, and individuals.

The contents of government publications are as varied as the departments, agencies, and bureaus which issue them. They include annual reports, transcripts of congressional hearings, statistical analyses, manuals of instruction, records of proceedings, bibliographies, directories, speeches, rules and regulations, results of research, and travel information.

They are printed or processed (that is, duplicated by mimeograph or other process), and they appear in almost every form: loose-leaf, unbound and bound books, pamphlets, leaflets, newspapers, periodicals, motion pictures, filmstrips, posters, and catalogs of art reproductions; some are examples of fine printing.

Some kinds of government publications are issued at all levels of government, but the chief source of government publications is the Federal government. It is said that the United States government is the largest single publisher in the world.

During the early years of our nation's history, printing was done by printers selected by Congress under a contract system. The publications of these contract printers were often poorly made, inadequately indexed, and sometimes not even identifiable as government publications.

In 1846, Congress created a Joint Committee on Printing, composed of three members from each house, to bring about reforms in printing practices. In 1852 a Superintendent of Public Printing was appointed to supervise the work of the printers who were selected under the contract system. The establishment of a national printing plant was authorized by Congress in 1860, and the United States government began doing its own printing in 1861.

The United States Government Printing Office is an independent body in the legislative branch of the government. The Public Printer, who is appointed by the President with the approval of the Senate, is responsible for the management of the Office. The Congressional Joint Committee on Printing has jurisdiction over the Government Printing Office in matters pertaining to the materials used in printing, wages of employees, and the efficient operation of the Office; it controls the arrangement and style of the *Congressional Record* and the *Congressional Directory*. The Superintendent of Documents (an office created in the Government Printing Office in 1895) is responsible for centralized distribution of government publications.

In carrying out the duties of his office, the Superintendent of Documents sells government publications to individuals, organizations, and institutions; distributes them to depository[1] libraries; compiles and distributes bibliographies and price lists; maintains a library and a reference catalog of all government publications; and provides information, upon request, about government publications.

Individuals may obtain certain government publications free, when available, from members of Congress or from the issuing agency, or they may purchase them from the Superintendent of Documents. Free price lists are issued by certain agencies and semimonthly lists of selected publications are available, free of charge, from the Superintendent of Documents.

Government publications provide primary source material in many areas, especially in statistics; in government operation; and in certain areas of the sciences, such as the results of scientific and medical research

[1] The distribution free of charge of Federal government publications to designated libraries was authorized by act of Congress, February 5, 1859. The law provides for one depository library for each congressional district in the United States and for two depositories at large for each state. All state libraries and the libraries of land-grant colleges and universities are named Federal depositories. Government publications in depository libraries are permanent and are available to the public, at least for reference use.

or patent and copyright applications. They are especially useful in history, the social sciences, education, personnel management, and the physical and biological sciences. Prepared by specialists who are in reality writing about their particular activities, they can be considered authoritative in the subjects they cover. They are up-to-date in that they present the latest information available to the agency which issues them. Many government publications provide bibliographies which are useful for further study and research. They are usually concise and readable.

Library users are often confused by the great number of government publications and do not know how to select or locate them. An understanding of the nature and purposes of government publications and of the ways in which these publications are organized and arranged for use in any given library will help to make these important resource materials more easily and quickly accessible.

There are several ways of organizing and arranging government publications.

1   They may be classified, cataloged, and shelved like other library materials.
2   They may be classified and cataloged like other library materials but kept in a special file or section of shelves.
3   They may be classified as Government Documents (or Government Publications) and arranged alphabetically or numerically on shelves or in vertical files.
4   Some government publications in a given library may be classified and cataloged like other library materials, and others in the same library may be treated as government publications and kept in a separate place.
5   They may be shelved without classification and arranged alphabetically by the issuing office.

If government publications are treated like other library materials, they will be assigned a number from the classification system in use in the library and will be arranged on the shelves according to the call number. In this case, the reader will locate them through the card catalog, just as he would locate any other kind of library material.

If they are classified according to the classification system in use in the library but are shelved together in a file or in a section of the library, the words "Gov. Doc.," or a similar symbol, will be added to the call number.

If they are not classified but are filed alphabetically or numerically, there will be a listing, an index, or a catalog nearby.

In general, the printed bibliographies or lists published by the Superintendent of Documents serve as an index to government publications when they are treated as a separate collection, as in a depository library. Instead of looking in the card catalog for a government publication, the student will consult a printed bibliography, such as the *Documents Catalog* or the *Monthly Catalog*, in much the same manner as he would a periodical index. The library may use these bibliographies as check lists of the items in its collection; in this case, the publications checked are those which the library has, and the printed symbol is both the classification and the location symbol. The symbol is a combination of letters of the alphabet, which designate the governmental agency which issued the publication, plus Arabic numerals, which designate the individual office and the kind of publication.

For example, the Defense Department is designated D from the first distinctive letter in the title, the Secretary of Defense is designated D 1, and all annual reports are given the symbol .1. Thus the symbol for the annual report of the Secretary of Defense is D 1.1.

Every item in the printed symbol is important, and every reference to the publication is important: the series, the type (whether leaflet, bulletin, circular, or monograph), and the year. It is necessary to copy all of them in order to locate a given publication in a library which uses this kind of organization (as well as in ordering a publication from the Superintendent of Documents).

The printed bibliographies provide descriptive and evaluative annotations for the publications listed and are useful in determining the kind of government publication to select for a particular problem.

In addition to the printed lists and bibliographies, there are reference works designed to aid the researcher in choosing government publications for particular purposes. Listed below are (1) printed lists and bibliographies which serve as indexes to government publications, and (2) reference works which are helpful in finding and using them.

Bibliographies *and* Lists

Ames, John G. *Comprehensive Index to the Publications of the United States Government, 1881–1893.* Washington, D.C.: Government Printing Office, 1905. 2 vols.

Poore, Benjamin Perley. *A Descriptive Catalogue of the Government Publications of the United States, September 5, 1774—to March 4, 1881.* Washington, D.C.: Government Printing Office, 1885.

U.S. Documents Office. *Catalog of the Public Documents of Congress and of All Departments of the Government of the United States for the Period from March 4, 1893 to December 31, 1940.* Washington, D.C.: Government Printing Office, 1896–1945. 25 vols.

U.S. Library of Congress, Division of Documents. *Monthly Checklist of State Publications.* Washington, D.C.: Government Printing Office, 1910– .

U.S. Superintendent of Documents. *United States Government Publications: Monthly Catalog.* Washington, D.C.: Government Printing Office, 1895– .

————. *Price Lists of Government Publications.* Washington, D.C.: Government Printing Office, 1898– .

————. *Selected United States Government Publications.* Washington, D.C.: Government Printing Office, 1928– .

Useful Reference Works

Boyd, Anne Morris, and Rips, Rae E. *United States Government Publications.* 3d ed. revised New York: The H. W. Wilson Company, 1950. Explains the nature, distribution, catalogs, and indexes of U.S. Government publications; lists and describes important publications of the departments of the U.S. Government: the executive, legislative, and judicial branches, Congress, the courts, etc.

Brown, Everett S. *Manual of Government Publications, United States and Foreign.* New York: Appleton-Century-Crofts, Inc., 1950. Emphasizes publications of American and British governments and those on international affairs.

Hirshberg, Herbert S., and Melinat, Carl H. *Subject Guide to United States Government Publications.* Chicago: American Library Association, 1947. Provides a means of finding important U.S. Government publications for information and reference.

Leidy, W. Philip. *A Popular Guide to Government Publications.* New York: Columbia University Press, 1953. Presents a compilation of government publications, popular in nature, which were issued from 1940 to 1950.

Schmeckebier, Laurence F., and Eastin, Roy B. *Government Publications and Their Use.* Revised ed. Washington, D.C.: The Brookings Institution, 1961. Includes new material relating to government periodicals and microprint reproductions of documents.

Wilcox, Jerome Kear. *Bibliography of New Guides and Aids to Public Documents Use, 1953–1956.* New York: Special Libraries Association, 1957. Includes international and general guides as well as guides to the use of municipal, state, and Federal publications.

PART FOUR

REFERENCE MATERIALS
IN THE SUBJECT FIELDS

CHAPTER FIFTEEN

SUBJECT REFERENCE MATERIALS

A GENERAL reference book, which has many subject specialists on its editorial staff, provides much information on the different subject fields; however, since the aim of the general reference book is to give wide and unrestricted coverage, specialized treatment of any one subject is necessarily limited.

For those persons who require more than general treatment of a specific subject, there are specialized reference books in every subject area.

A subject reference book can be defined as a publication in which items of information about one particular subject—literature, history, music, sports, education—are brought together from many sources and arranged so that individual items can be found quickly and easily.

Subject reference books introduce the student (or layman) to the subject matter of the different branches of knowledge.

1   They provide specialized definitions not found in general dictionaries for the words and phrases in a given field.

2 They trace the growth of important ideas in a subject area.

3 They provide an introduction to the development of the literature of the subject.

4 They give authoritative information on major questions and issues in a specialized area.

5 They explain and clarify concepts.

6 They locate, describe, and evaluate the literature of the field.

7 They provide facts which indicate trends, and they summarize the events of a given year in a given subject field.

Subject reference books are adapted to the peculiar characteristics of the subject under consideration. For example, in music there are dictionaries of musical themes and musical scores; in art, catalogs of reproductions and auctions; and in science, handbooks of tables and formulas.

KINDS AND PURPOSES OF SUBJECT REFERENCE BOOKS

The kinds of reference books in each subject field are the same as those in the general area, and they serve similar purposes on a more restricted scale.

1 Bibliographies and guides
   a Point out the literature of the field in question
   b Indicate works which may not be in the library and therefore serve as aids to further search
   c Provide descriptive and evaluative information which the catalog card cannot include
   d Arrange works according to form: dictionaries, histories, encyclopedias, handbooks, indexes, and books of criticism (if the subject field is literature)

2 Indexes
   a Indicate where periodical articles on a subject can be found
   b Indicate collections in which plays, short stories, essays, and poems can be found
   c Analyze books and parts of books

3 Dictionaries
   a Provide specialized definitions and explanations of terminology and concepts
   b Help to establish terminology
   c Serve as a guide to current as well as historical usage of words and phrases
   d Give short, concise answers to questions
   e May give chronology
   f May give biographical information
   g May give pronunciation
4 Encyclopedias
   a Give a "summary treatment" of the different phases and aspects of a subject
   b Explain historical backgrounds, trends, and the influence of events outside the subject area, such as the influence of social conditions on the literature of a period
   c Trace the development of ideas in a subject field
5 Handbooks
   a Identify references, allusions, dates, quotations, and characters in literature
   b Summarize literary plots
   c Provide statistics and useful bits of information
6 Yearbooks and annuals
   a Summarize events of the past year, including research projects undertaken and completed
   b Provide a source for hard-to-locate items of information
7 Collections (anthologies)
   a Bring together in one place selections or quotations from essays, poetry, drama, short stories, periodicals, and other forms of literature
   b Serve as source materials for courses in literature, history, education, psychology and other subject fields
8 Atlases and gazetteers
   a Provide geographical information in any subject area, and may give maps
   b Give over-all picture emphasizing location of industries, products, literature

9   Biographical dictionaries
   a   Provide concise information about important persons in a subject field: authors, scholars, scientists, educators
   b   May include bibliographies and evaluations of an author's work
10   Reference histories give factual information, trends, and main facts of development, covering
   a   Chronology
   b   Interpretation of events
   c   Biographical data
   d   Bibliographical information
11   Professional journals provide up-to-date articles, essays, book reviews, and other material relating specifically to the subject matter of a given branch of knowledge

The choice of a reference book in a subject field, as in a general area, depends upon the nature of the question to be answered: (1) the kind of information required, (2) the subject area of which it is a part, and (3) the factors affecting the question, such as time and location.

USING A SUBJECT REFERENCE BOOK

Efficient use of a subject reference book is dependent upon an understanding of (1) the purposes of each kind of subject reference book, (2) the organization and the arrangement of the material, and (3) the distinguishing features of each book. Before using a subject reference book, one should examine the table of contents and the preliminary pages which explain the purpose, the plan and arrangement, and any special features of the book.

The succeeding chapters introduce the several subject areas and present representative reference books in each area. The subject fields discussed are the major classes of knowledge as they are organized in the Dewey Decimal Classification System. With one exception, they are presented in the order in which they appear in the classification scheme; the exception is that history is discussed with the social sciences. Not all the reference books discussed in the preceding paragraphs are found in each subject field; however, the examples which are given in the succeeding chapters appear in the order in which they are discussed above.

Since new reference books and new editions of old ones are being published continually, it is necessary to consult the card catalog frequently in order to keep up-to-date on the reference materials in the library. The titles listed here are only suggestions, for they represent but a small portion of the thousands that are available. Each reader will supplement them and, in time, replace them with new publications.

CHAPTER SIXTEEN

PHILOSOPHY AND PSYCHOLOGY

THE Dewey Decimal Classification begins with the general and works toward the specific. Within the specific classes, it begins with the general and goes into the particular.

PHILOSOPHY

The first subject class in the Dewey Decimal System, as well as in the Library of Congress System, is Philosophy, historically the most general science, the science of sciences. Deriving from two Greek words, *philein*, to love, and *sophia*, wisdom, philosophy has been thought of both as the seeking of wisdom and as the wisdom sought.

Originally, philosophy meant the general principles under which all facts could be explained; it comprised all learning except technical rules and the practical arts. In the medieval universities, philosophy was the omnibus subject which covered the whole body of sciences and the liberal arts. This comprehensive meaning is carried forward into the present in the academic degree doctor of philosophy (Ph.D.).

In the broadest academic sense, philosophy is the critical investigation and the organization of all knowledge drawn from any source; also, it consists in raising reasoned questions about matters and problems in areas of life where exact knowledge (at a particular time) is not possible. Many of the questions of philosophy have passed over into the subject of science as man's exact knowledge has spread and advanced. In brief, the purpose of the broad and persistent speculations and questions of philosophy has been, and is, to understand the world.

In a less academic sense, philosophy represents an organized and more-than-less consistent personal point of view or attitude toward life, reality, and value, as, for example, George Bernard Shaw's philosophy as expressed in his dramatic works or Robert Frost's philosophy as shown in his poetry.

The basic literature of philosophy is the writings of the philosophers themselves and critical commentaries upon these writings. Thus it can be said that there is no such thing as an "established" philosophy; there are only philosophers and their philosophies. The great philosophers of the ages run the gamut of the alphabet from Aquinas and Aristotle, through Descartes, Dewey, Hegel, and Kant, to Russell, Santayana, Sartre, and Whitehead. The systems of ideas, theories, speculations, and principles of life, reality, values, and destiny which these great thinkers and others like them have developed are designated by such names as idealism, pragmatism, realism, rationalism, naturalism, positivism, absolutism, instrumentalism, and existentialism. The special areas or branches into which these and other systems of philosophical thought are divided include metaphysics, epistemology, logic, ethics, and aesthetics.

The number of helpful reference works in philosophy is limited.

REFERENCE BOOKS AND BOOKS ON HISTORY OF PHILOSOPHY

Bibliographies and Indexes[1]

Essays and General Literature Index, 1934– . Indexes collections of essays and other literature which have reference value for philosophy.

[1] See also Chapter Thirteen, Bibliographies.

International Index to Periodical Literature, 1907– . Indexes periodicals in the field of philosophy.

Dictionaries and Encyclopedias

Baldwin, James Mark (ed.). *Dictionary of Philosophy and Psychology.* New ed. New York: The Macmillan Company, 1925. 3 vols. (Reprinted by Peter Smith, 1946.) Out of date for modern developments, but still useful; covers the entire field.

Runes, Dagobert D. (ed.). *The Dictionary of Philososphy.* New York: Philosophical Library, Inc., 1942. Gives concise definitions and explains philosophical terms covering the entire range of philosophical thought.

Urmson, J. O. (ed.). *The Concise Encyclopedia of Western Philosophy and Philosophers.* New York: Hawthorn Books, Inc., 1960. Provides analytical biographical articles on philosophy from Abelard to the present time and gives discussions of specific topics; has up-to-date bibliographies; includes portraits.

Biographical Dictionaries[2]

Runes, Dagobert D. (ed.). *Who's Who in Philosophy.* Vol. I. New York: Philosophical Library, Inc., 1942. Lists Anglo-American philosophers.

Histories of Philosophy

Clark, Gordon H. *Thales to Dewey: A History of Philosophy.* Boston: Houghton Mifflin Company, 1957.

Durant, Will. *The Story of Philosophy.* Revised ed. New York: Simon and Schuster, Inc., 1933.

Miller, Hugh. *An Historical Introduction to Modern Philosophy.* New York: The Macmillan Company, 1947.

Russell, Bertrand. *A History of Western Philosophy.* New York: Simon and Schuster, Inc., 1945.

Schneider, Herbert W. *A History of American Philosophy.* New York: Columbia University Press, 1946.

[2] See also Chapter Ten, Biographical Dictionaries.

Webb, Clement Charles Julian. *A History of Philosophy*. (The Home University Library.) New York: Henry Holt and Company, Inc., 1915.

PSYCHOLOGY

Psychology, from the Greek word *psyche,* meaning mind or soul, plus *logos,* meaning law, has been historically the science which treats of the mind in any of its aspects—function, organization and structure, and effect on behavior. Once a part of philosophy and still a close companion, psychology developed and became a separate branch of learning within the past century.

In recent times, psychology has been thought of as the serious study of the organism as an individual whole, as the study of the organism and its activities rather than of physiological functions. For example, the study of the functions of the brain is thought of more as a physiological than as a psychological theme. Thus the general theme of psychology is the study of the activities of the total organism (man and lower animal) in its interrelations with its physical environment and with its social setting and influences.

Psychology is often referred to and identified in terms of a school or system, as, for example, behaviorist psychology, or Gestalt psychology.

Perhaps the best and most comprehensive way in which to see modern psychology is through an acquaintance with some of its many subdivisions, which are determined by, and are named to describe, the kinds of problems studied. These kinds and fields of psychological study are so connected that one should not try to arrange them either chronologically or in order of their current importance. Some of the more important subdivisions of psychology are abnormal, analytic, animal, applied, experimental, genetic, motor, and physiological. Other subdivisions of psychology are child, adolescent, adult, educational, social, and industrial. Other fields of inquiry which draw heavily upon the basic concepts, principles, and experience-findings of medicine, religion, education, physiology, and sociology are psychiatry, psychoanalysis, psychotherapy, and psychopathology.

Bibliography[3]

Boring, Edwin G. (ed.). *Harvard List of Books in Psychology.* Cambridge, Mass.: Harvard University Press, 1955. *Supplement.* 1958.

Indexes and Abstracts

Annual Review of Psychology. Stanford, Calif.: Annual Reviews, Inc., 1950– . Reviews contemporary psychological literature; presents critical appraisals of current research and theory in the most active and general fields.

Education Index.

International Index.

Psychological Abstracts. Washington, D.C.: American Psychological Association, 1927– . (Monthly.) Contains a bibliographical listing of new books and articles, grouped by subject, with a signed abstract of each one.

Dictionaries and Encyclopedias

Encyclopaedia of the Social Sciences.[4] Includes subjects related to psychology.

English, Horace Bidwell, and English, Ava C. (eds.). *A Compound Dictionary of Psychological and Psychoanalytical Terms.* New York: Longmans, Green & Co., Inc., 1958. Gives definitions of all terms that are used frequently in a specialized or technical sense; is not encyclopedic.

Harriman, Philip Lawrence (ed.). *Encyclopedia of Psychology.* New York: Philosophical Library, Inc., 1956. Emphasizes important trends in contemporary psychology; provides comprehensive bibliographies.

Harris, Chester W., and Liba, Marie R. (eds.). *Encyclopedia of Educational Research.*[4]

Monroe, Paul (ed.). *A Cyclopedia of Education.*[4]

Warren, Howard C. (ed.). *Dictionary of Psychology.* Boston: Houghton Mifflin Company, 1934. Includes both English and foreign terminology and extensive bibliographies.

---

[3] See also Chapter Thirteen, Bibliographies.

[4] See Chapter Eighteen for bibliographical description and annotation and for other materials which are useful in the field of psychology.

Biographical Dictionaries and Directories[5]

American Men of Science. 9th ed. Vol. III. Includes living persons in the field of psychology
Leaders in Education.
Murchison, Carl (ed.). *The Psychological Register.* Vols. II and III. Worcester, Mass.: Clark University Press, 1929. Universal; arranged by country; lists the writings of each biographee.

Professional Journals in Philosophy and Psychology

American Journal of Psychology. 1887–   . (Quarterly.)
Journal of General Psychology. 1928–   . (Quarterly.)
Journal of Philosophy. 1904–   . (Fortnightly.)
Journal of the History of Ideas. 1940–   . (Quarterly.)
Modern Schoolman. 1925–   . (Quarterly.)
Philosophical Review. 1892–   . (Quarterly.)
Psychological Review. 1894–   . (Bimonthly.)

[5] See also Chapter Ten, Biographical Dictionaries.

CHAPTER SEVENTEEN

RELIGION AND MYTHOLOGY

THE second subject class in the Dewey Decimal System is assigned to Religion. This class embraces all religions, including pagan religions and mythology.

RELIGION

There are many religions and many definitions of religion.

Religion might perhaps be defined, very generally, as belief in a fourth dimension—a dimension which takes us out of material space, where everything changes, disorder reigns, and we are lonely and unhappy to attain *something which is,* a Being who exists absolutely, in all perfection and splendor. To feel that we are bound to that Being, that we are dependent on Him, to aspire to find Him, to hunger and thirst after Him: that is the religious sense.[1]

Religion . . . a system of beliefs and practices having reference to man's relation with God . . . .[2]

. . . In essence religion is related to the beliefs concerning some ruling force or forces and the ways in which these forces are worshipped and obeyed.[3]

In extent and variety, religious literature is perhaps the largest subject class. The study of books and libraries (Chapter One) revealed that the earliest records of every civilization are religious or moral works. Temple records constitute the first historical annals.

In addition to the basic Scriptures of each religion, there are many kinds of religious literature, including historical studies, devotional and inspirational literature, church doctrines and works of interpretation, lives of the saints, digests of ecclesiastical law, church rituals, and informational literature.

The reference books in the field of religion, like all other reference books, are compilations of factual information and are planned to answer specific questions about religions and the literature of the various religions. These reference books include dictionaries and encyclopedias, biographical dictionaries, concordances,[4] directories, yearbooks, and indexes.

REPRESENTATIVE REFERENCE BOOKS IN RELIGION

Indexes[5]

The Catholic Periodical Index.
Essay and General Literature Index.

[1] André-Jean Festugière, *Personal Religion among the Greeks* (Berkeley, Calif.: University of California Press, 1954), p. 1.

[2] Donald Attwater (ed.), *The Catholic Encyclopaedic Dictionary* (New York: The Macmillan Company, 1958), p. 449. Used with their permission.

[3] Lester Asheim, *The Humanities and the Library* (Chicago: American Library Association, 1957), p. 3.

[4] A concordance lists, in alphabetical order and in context, the principal or key words in a book or in the works of an author.

[5] See also Chapter Ten, Bibliographies.

International Index.
Readers' Guide to Periodical Literature.

Concordances

Cruden, Alexander (comp.). *A Complete Concordance to the Holy Scriptures of the Old and New Testaments.* New ed. Westwood, N.J.: Fleming H. Revell Company, n.d. Includes a concordance to the Apocrypha.

Joy, Charles R. (comp.). *Harper's Topical Concordance.* New York: Harper & Brothers, 1940. Indexes the King James Version by topics.

Nelson's Complete Concordance of the Revised Standard Version of the Bible. Compiled under the supervision of John W. Ellison. New York: Thomas Nelson & Sons, 1957. Gives context and location of each key word.

Thompson, Newton Wayland, and Stock, Raymond (comps.). *Complete Concordance to the Bible (Douay Version).* St. Louis: B. Herder Book Company, 1945. Indexes the actual words of the Douay Roman Catholic Version of the Bible.

Dictionaries

Attwater, Donald (ed.). *The Catholic Encyclopaedic Dictionary.* New York: The Macmillan Company, 1958. Defines and explains terms, names, and phrases in the theology, philosophy, canon law, and liturgy of the Catholic Church; includes biographies of the saints in the general calendar of the Roman Catholic Church.

Cross, F. L. (ed.). *Oxford Dictionary of the Christian Church.* New York: Oxford University Press, 1957. Covers historical developments, doctrine, definitions, biography; is addressed to the educated public.

Mathews, Shailer, and Smith, Gerald B. (eds.). *A Dictionary of Religion and Ethics.* New York: The Macmillan Company, 1923. Defines and discusses the terminology of religion and ethics; gives biographies of persons not living.

Miller, Madeleine S., and Miller, J. Lane. *Harper's Bible Dictionary.* 6th ed. New York: Harper & Brothers, 1959. Addressed to all levels of readers; provides maps and illustrations.

Encyclopedias

The Catholic Encyclopedia. New York: Catholic Encyclopedia Press, 1907–1922. 17 vols. *Supplement II.* Edited by Vincent C. Hopkins. New York: Gilmary Society, 1954. (Loose leaf; new edition in progress.) A monographic encyclopedia; not limited to subjects of interest only to Catholics; makes notable contributions to the literature of science, philosophy, civil and ecclesiastical law, education, music, and art. Vol. 17 is a supplement.

Ferm, Vergilius (ed.). *An Encyclopedia of Religion.* New York: Philosophical Library, Inc., 1945. Gives definitions, historical background, bibliography, and the theology of the major religions.

Hastings, James (ed.). *Encyclopaedia of Religion and Ethics.* New York: Charles Scribner's Sons, 1908–1927. 12 vols. and index. Contains articles on all religions, all of the great ethical systems and movements, religious beliefs and customs, philosophical ideas, moral practices, and important persons and places.

The Jewish Encyclopedia. New York: Funk & Wagnalls Company, 1901–1906. 12 vols. Records the history, religion, literature, and customs of the Jewish people from the beginning to the present time; includes biography and bibliography.

Mayer, Frederick Emanuel (ed.). *The Religious Bodies of America.* 2d ed. St. Louis: Concordia Publishing House, 1956. Treats the historical development, doctrines, and practices of the churches of America.

The New Schaff-Herzog Encyclopedia of Religious Knowledge. Based on 3d ed. Grand Rapids, Mich.: Baker Book House, 1951. 13 vols. Covers Biblical, historical, doctrinal, and practical theology from the earliest times to the present; includes biography.

Roth, Cecil (ed.). *The Standard Jewish Encyclopedia.* New York: Doubleday & Company, Inc., 1959. A one-volume work; places emphasis on Israel and America; useful for articles on modern Hebrew life and culture; includes biography of living persons.

Zaehner, Robert Charles (ed.). *The Concise Encyclopedia of Living Faiths.* New York: Hawthorn Books, Inc., 1959. Covers living faiths only; illustrated.

Yearbooks

American Jewish Yearbook, 5660– . September 5, 1899– .
Northern Baptist Convention Yearbook. 1941– .
Official Catholic Directory. 1886– .
Southern Baptist Handbook. 1921– .
Yearbook of the Congregational Christian Churches of the United States of America. 1879– .
Yearbook of American Churches. 1916– .

Biographical Dictionaries

See dictionaries and encyclopedias of religion and general encyclopedias and biographical dictionaries.

MYTHOLOGY

Mythology is a collective word, usually thought of by social anthropologists as including the stories and tales (myths) which describe the origin, nature, and adventures of the gods and goddesses of a people. In other words, myths are concerned with the supernatural and are especially associated with religious feasts, festivals, rites, and beliefs. For this reason, mythology is often classified by social scientists as a part of primitive religion. Both mythology and religion have their beginnings beyond recorded history.

REPRESENTATIVE REFERENCE BOOKS IN MYTHOLOGY

Bulfinch's Mythology. New York: Thomas Y. Crowell Company, 1947. Covers "age of fable, age of chivalry, and the legends of Charlemagne."

Frazer, Sir James (ed.). *The Golden Bough: A Study in Magic and Religion.* 3d ed. revised. New York: St. Martin's Press, Inc., 1955. 12 vols. A comprehensive collection of information about primitive religions: traces many myths and rites to their prehistoric beginnings.

Gray, Louis Herbert (ed.). *The Mythology of All Races, Greek and Roman.* 26th ed. Boston: Marshall Jones Company, 1958. 13 vols. Includes text and illustrations.

Hastings, James (ed.). *Encyclopaedia of Religion and Ethics.* Has articles on mythology and folklore.

Larousse Encyclopedia of Mythology. New York: Prometheus Press, 1959. Covers world mythology; is divided by nationalities.

CHAPTER EIGHTEEN

HISTORY, THE SOCIAL SCIENCES, AND EDUCATION

The discovery of writing and the beginnings of the measurement of time made possible the preservation of temple records which form the first historical annals.[1]

HISTORY is that area of study which is concerned with the recording of past events and with the interpretations of the relationships and significance of these events. It is divided into ancient, medieval, and modern, and each of these divisions may be subdivided geographically, as the history of medieval Europe or the history of modern England. History can be subdivided further into its economic, cultural, social, political, military, and literary aspects. The History class (900) of the Dewey Decimal System includes, as related subject areas, biography and geography.

[1] T. R. Glover, "Historiography: Antiquity," *Encyclopaedia of the Social Sciences*, VII (1932), p. 368.

Biography is that form of history which is applied to individuals rather than to nations or to cultures (see Chapter Ten).

Geography, from *geo*, the combining form of Greek for earth, plus *graphia*, writing, is the science concerned with the description of the earth's surface, of its form and physical features, of its natural and political subdivisions, and of its climate, products, and population. It is frequently divided into mathematical, physical, and political geography.

Many of the general reference books—encyclopedias, dictionaries, handbooks, atlases, gazetteers, indexes, and bibliographies—provide material in the field of history. There are, however, specialized reference books that have been prepared for the primary purpose of aiding students of history. They include bibliographies, guides, indexes, encyclopedias, chronologies, handbooks, dictionaries, historical atlases, and general histories.

In addition to atlases and gazetteers, which are recognized as being essential aids in the study of geography, there are bibliographies of, and indexes to, the literature of geography, dictionaries of place names and of terminology, and guidebooks which provide descriptive material and maps not usually found in gazetteers and atlases.

The social sciences[2] comprise those branches of knowledge which have to do with the activities of the individual as a member of society. Included in the Social Sciences class of the Dewey Decimal System (300) are sociology, statistics, political science, economics, law, government, social welfare, education,[3] public service and utilities, and customs and folklore.[4]

There are numerous reference books devoted to the subject matter of the several social sciences. They include bibliographies, guides, indexes, dictionaries, encyclopedias, handbooks, yearbooks, biographical dictionaries, directories, and atlases.

---

[2] The social sciences are not to be confused with "social studies," which are portions of the subject matter of the social sciences suitable for study in the elementary and secondary schools and are developed into courses of study which place emphasis on social aims.

[3] Education as a subject field is discussed on pp. 161–165.

[4] For a full discussion of the social sciences, see Edwin R. A. Seligman, "What Are the Social Sciences?" *Encyclopaedia of the Social Sciences*, I (1930), 3–7.

REPRESENTATIVE REFERENCE BOOKS IN HISTORY
AND THE SOCIAL SCIENCES

General

GUIDES AND INDEXES

Hoselitz, Bert F. (ed.). *A Reader's Guide to the Social Sciences*. Glencoe, Ill.: Free Press, 1959. Presents a general introduction, in discussion form, to the literature of the social sciences; traces the development of the social sciences in the last 200 years.

International Index. New York: The H. W. Wilson Company, 1907– . (Quarterly.) A guide to periodical literature in the social sciences and humanities; includes periodicals published in the United States, Great Britain, and Canada.

Readers' Guide to Periodical Literature.

Education Index.

Cumulative Book Index.

DICTIONARIES AND ENCYCLOPEDIAS

Seligman, Edwin R. A., and Johnson, Alvin (eds.). *Encyclopaedia of the Social Sciences*. New York: The Macmillan Company, 1930–1935. 15 vols. Provides articles on all of the social sciences, bringing out the relationships of each science to all other relevant sciences.

The Worldmark Encyclopedia of the Nations. New York: Harper & Brothers, 1960. A practical guide to the geography, history, political, social, and economic status of all nations, their international relationships and the United Nations system (subtitle).

Zadrozny, John T. (ed.). *Dictionary of Social Science*. Washington, D.C.: Public Affairs Press, 1959. For social scientists and laymen; gives actual usages of the more important terms in the major social sciences.

BIOGRAPHICAL DICTIONARIES

Cattell, Jacques (ed.). *American Men of Science*. 9th ed. New York: R. R. Bowker Company, 1956. Vol. III, *The Social and Behavioral Sciences*, provides brief biographical information about persons in geography, anthropology, and other social sciences.

Directory of American Scholars.

History

BIBLIOGRAPHIES AND GUIDES

American Historical Association. *Guide to Historical Literature.* George Frederick Howe, Chairman, Board of Editors. New York: The Macmillan Company, 1961. Successor to Dutcher, *Guide to Historical Literature;* follows the same general arrangement.

Dutcher, George Matthew, and Others (eds.). *Guide to Historical Literature.* New York: The Macmillan Company, 1931. A selective bibliography, arranged by large subject and country headings; indexes reviews in professional journals.

Handlin, Oscar, and Others (eds.). *Guide to American History.* Boston: Belknap Press of Harvard University, 1954. Addressed to the intelligent general reader, student, and scholar; gives a selection of material in political, social, constitutional, and economic history.

Library of Congress, Reference Division. *A Guide to the Study of the United States of America.* Washington, D.C.: U.S. Government Printing Office, 1960. [Introduces] representative books reflecting the development of American life and thought (subtitle).

DICTIONARIES AND ENCYCLOPEDIAS

Adams, James Truslow (ed.). *Dictionary of American History.* 2d ed. revised. New York: Charles Scribner's Sons, 1942. 5 vols. and index. Not encyclopedic; has short, signed articles.

Keller, Helen Rex. *Dictionary of Dates.* New York: The Macmillan Company, 1934. 2 vols. Arranged by country, then chronologically; outlines historical events through 1930.

Langer, William L. (ed.). *An Encyclopedia of World History.* Revised ed. Boston: Houghton Mifflin Company, 1952. Covers ancient, medieval, and modern history; is arranged chronologically.

Morris, Richard B. (ed.). *Encyclopedia of American History.* New York: Harper & Brothers, 1955. Gives essential historical facts about American life and institutions in both chronological and topical arrangements; includes brief biographical information about notable Americans.

Woodcock, Percival George (ed.). *Concise Dictionary of Ancient History.* New York: Philosophical Library, Inc., 1955. Covers the period from the beginning of recorded history to the fall of Rome, with emphasis on Greek and Roman history.

HISTORICAL ATLASES

Adams, James Truslow (ed.). *Atlas of American History*. New York: Charles Scribner's Sons, 1943. Companion volume to *Dictionary of American History*.

Heyden, A. A. M. Van Der, and Scullard, H. H. (eds.). *Atlas of the Classical World*. New York: Thomas Nelson & Sons, 1959. Includes maps, illustrations, and text relating to the religious, economic, military, literary, artistic, and political history of Greece and Rome.

Lord, Clifford L., and Lord, Elizabeth H. (eds.). *Historical Atlas of the United States*. Revised ed., New York: Henry Holt and Company, Inc., 1953. Provides maps of the political and economic history, population, and natural resources of the United States to 1950.

Palmer, R. R. (ed.). *Atlas of World History*. Chicago: Rand McNally & Company, 1957. Covers, in maps, the history of the world; has a number of political and social maps.

Shepherd, William R. (ed.). *Historical Atlas*. 8th revised ed. New York: Barnes & Noble, Inc., 1956. Provides maps of world history from 1450 B.C. to the present.

REFERENCE HISTORIES

Cambridge Ancient History. New York: Cambridge University Press, 1929–1939. 12 vols. 5 vols. of plates.

Cambridge Mediaeval History. New York: Cambridge University Press, 1911–1936. 8 vols.

Cambridge Modern History. New York: Cambridge University Press, 1902–1922. 13 vols. and atlas.

PROFESSIONAL JOURNALS

American Heritage. 1949–   . (Bimonthly.)
American Historical Review. 1895–   . (Quarterly.)
English Historical Review. 1886–   . (Quarterly.)

Geography

BIBLIOGRAPHIES AND GUIDES

Wright, John K., and Platt, Elizabeth (eds.). *Aids to Geographical Research*. 2d ed. completely revised. New York: Columbia University Press for the American Geographical Society, 1947. Lists and describes the literature of the field.

ATLASES[5]

Bartholomew, John W. (ed.). *Advanced Atlas of Modern Geography*. 3d ed. New York: McGraw-Hill Book Company, Inc., 1957.

———. *The Times Atlas of the World*. Mid-century ed. London: The Times Publishing Company, Ltd., 1955–1959.

Encyclopaedia Britannica World Atlas. Chicago: Encyclopaedia Britannica, Inc., 1960.

Espenshade, Edward B. (ed.). *Goode's World Atlas*. 11th ed. Chicago: Rand McNally & Company, 1960.

Hammond's Ambassador World Atlas. Maplewood, N.J.: C. S. Hammond & Company, 1954.

Rand McNally Standard World Atlas. Chicago: Rand McNally & Company, 1958.

GAZETTEERS[5]

Collocott, T. C., and Thorne, J. O. (eds.). *Macmillan World Gazetteer and Geographical Dictionary*. Revised ed. New York: The Macmillan Company, 1957.

Seltzer, Leon E. (ed.). *Columbia-Lippincott Gazetteer of the World*. New York: Columbia University Press, 1952.

Webster's Geographical Dictionary. Revised ed. Springfield, Mass.: G. & C. Merriam Company, 1959.

PROFESSIONAL JOURNALS

Economic Geography. 1925– . (Quarterly.)
Geographical Review. 1916– . (Quarterly.)
Journal of Geography. 1902– . (Monthly except June and August.)

The Social Sciences

BIBLIOGRAPHIES AND GUIDES

Coman, E. T. *Sources of Business Information*. Englewood Cliffs, N.J.: Prentice-Hall, Inc., 1949. Lists bibliographies, manuals, textbooks, periodicals—chiefly American.

Forrester, Gertrude (ed.). *Occupational Literature*. New York: The H. W. Wilson Company, 1958. Provides an annotated bibliography of books and pamphlets; arranged alphabetically by occupation.

N. W. Ayer & Son's Directory of Newspapers and Periodicals. Philadelphia: N. W. Ayer & Son, Inc., 1880– . Serves as a guide to American

[5] See Chapter Eleven for annotations of atlases and gazetteers.

towns and cities, their principal industries, publications, and means of transportation.

Business Periodicals Index. New York: The H. W. Wilson Company, 1958– . (Monthly except July.) One of the two indexes which succeeded the *Industrial Arts Index* in January, 1958; indexes by subject periodicals in business and related fields.

Cumulative Book Index. 1898– . Indexes by author, title, and subject current books in the English language published in all countries.

Index to Legal Periodicals. New York: The H. W. Wilson Company for the American Association of Law Libraries, 1908– . (Monthly except August.) Indexes by author and subject legal periodicals and reports of bar associations and judicial councils.

Industrial Arts Index. 1913–1957. Includes periodical articles on business and finance.

Occupational Index. New York: New York University, 1936– . (Quarterly.) Lists and abstracts current publications on occupational subjects.

Public Affairs Information Service Bulletin. New York: Public Affairs Information Service, 1915–. (Weekly.) A subject guide to the current literature in the field of the social sciences; includes books, documents, periodical articles.

Fairchild, Henry Pratt (ed.). *Dictionary of Sociology*. New York: Philosophical Library, Inc., 1944. Gives specialized and authoritative definitions in the field of sociology.

Horton, Byrne J., and Others (eds.). *Dictionary of Modern Economics*. Washington, D.C.: Public Affairs Press, 1948. Defines terms; presents important factors affecting economics, including Supreme Court decisions; gives bibliography and biography.

Lazarus, Harold (ed.). *American Business Dictionary*. New York: Philosophical Library, Inc., 1957. Presents a business vocabulary to meet the daily needs of those who work and write in that area.

Nemmers, Erwin E., and Janzen, Cornelius C. (eds.). *Dictionary of Economics and Business*. Paterson, N.J.: Littlefield, Adams & Company, 1959. Covers terms used in college courses in business and economics.

Palgrave's Dictionary of Political Economy. Edited by Henry Higgs. London: Macmillan & Co., Ltd., 1923–1926. 3 vols. Provides an overview of economic thought; shows development of economic thought and study in England, the United States, and other English-speaking countries.

Sloan, Harold S., and Zurcher, Arnold J. (eds.). *Dictionary of Economics.* Revised ed. New York: Barnes & Nobles, Inc., 1957. Contains definitions and explanations of economic terms in all phases of economics; includes digests of relevant American statutes.

Smith, Edward C., and Zurcher, Arnold J. (eds.). *New Dictionary of American Politics.* Revised ed. New York: Barnes & Noble, Inc., 1955. Defines terms in general use in the field of American politics and state, county, and city government.

HANDBOOKS

The Book of States. Chicago: The Council of State Government, 1935– . (Biennial.) Contains authoritative information on state governments, officials, services, organizations, and methods of financing them.

Economic Almanac. New York: National Industrial Conference Board, Inc., 1940– . (Annual.) Provides useful facts about business, labor, and government in the United States and in other countries.

Political Handbook of the World. New York: Council on Foreign Relations, Inc., 1927– . (Annual.) Gives information on government, government officials, party leaders, political events, and newspapers.

South American Handbook. London: Trade and Travel Publications, 1924– . (Annual.) Covers South and Central America; presents information about government, transportation, communication, natural resources.

Taintor, Sarah A., and Munro, Kate M. (eds.). *The Secretary's Handbook.* 8th ed. Completely revised by Kate M. Munro. New York: The Macmillan Company, 1958. Gives rules and correct form in letter writing; is a manual of correct usage.

YEARBOOKS AND ANNUALS[6]

The American Yearbook. 1910–1919, 1925– . New York: Thomas Nelson & Sons, 1929– . Records events and progress in science, the social sciences, and the humanities; covers all countries, but places emphasis on the United States.

Social Work Yearbook. New York: Russell Sage Foundation, 1930– . (Biennial.) Describes organized activities in social work and related fields.

The Statesman's Yearbook. London: Macmillan & Co., Ltd., 1864– . (Annual.) Presents a statistical and historical picture of the world for a given year.

U.S. Bureau of the Census. *Statistical Abstract of the United States.* Washington, D.C.: U.S. Government Printing Office, 1878– . Summarizes

[6] See also Chapter Twelve, Yearbooks and Handbooks.

statistics of all political, social, industrial, and economic organizations of the United States; includes bibliography.

Yearbook of the United Nations. New York: United Nations, Department of Public Information, 1947– . Provides a comprehensive account of the activities of the United Nations and its related intergovernmental agencies.

The Yearbook of World Affairs. Published under the auspices of the London Institute of World Affairs. New York: Frederick A. Praeger, Inc., 1947– . Gives long articles on subjects in the social sciences

ATLASES[7]

Van Royen, William (ed.). *Atlas of the World's Resources.* Vol. 1: *The Agricultural Resources of the World.* Vol. II: *The Mineral Resources of the World* (by William Van Royen and Oliver Bowles). Englewood Cliffs, N.J.: Prentice-Hall, Inc., for the University of Maryland, 1952–1954. Gives an overview of the geographical distribution of the world's agricultural products, and presents the world situation with respect to mineral output and reserves; includes maps and graphs.

BIOGRAPHICAL DICTIONARIES[8]

American Men of Science. 9th ed. Vol. 3.
Directory of American Scholars.
Who's Who in American Education.

PROFESSIONAL JOURNALS

American Political Science Review. 1906– . (Quarterly.)
Annals of the American Academy of Political and Social Science. 1890– . (Bimonthly.)
Journal of Educational Sociology. 1927– . (Monthly, September to May.)
Journal of Political Economy. 1892– . (Bimonthly.)
Social Education. 1937– . (Monthly, October to May.)

EDUCATION

The word "education" has several meanings, and it is necessary to make clear its meaning as a *subject field* before beginning a study of reference materials in this area. A brief statement of two of the several meanings of education will help to clarify its meaning as a branch of knowledge.

---

[7] See also Chapter Eleven, Atlases and Gazetteers.
[8] See also Chapter Ten, Biographical Dictionaries.

In the broad sense, education is the sum total of all of the ways, both formal and informal, by which a person develops attitudes, abilities, and behavior patterns and acquires knowledge.

In another and less broad sense, education is the social process by which people are placed under the influence of an organized and controlled environment, such as a school, in the hope that they will attain more rapidly and effectively their fullest possible development as individuals and will learn how to live as competent citizens in their society. Elementary school, high school, and college are some of the stages in this controlled process.

Education, as a subject field, that is, as a branch of knowledge, is the science which has to do with the principles and practices of teaching and learning. It is the name given to that curriculum in institutions of higher education which consists of professional courses for the preparation of teachers, supervisors, and administrators. Included in these courses are philosophy and history of education (that is, as a social process), psychology as applied to learning and teaching, curriculum, methods of teaching (how to teach), administration, and supervision.

The following reference books are designed to answer, in the language of the educator, some of the numerous and specialized questions in this subject field. This is only a sample of the books available.

BIBLIOGRAPHIES, GUIDES, AND INDEXES

Alexander, Carter, and Burke, Arvid J. *How to Locate Educational Information and Data.* 4th ed. New York: Bureau of Publications, Teachers College, Columbia University, 1958. Lists materials in the field of education and tells how to use them; explains methods in library research; designed for graduate students in education but is useful to the undergraduate.

Association of American Colleges. *A Guide to Graduate Study: Programs Leading to the Ph.D. Degree.* 2d ed. Edited by Frederick W. Ness. Washington, D.C.: Association of American Colleges, 1960. Describes graduate schools as to size, admission requirements, fees, and fields of study for the Ph.D. degree.

Children's Catalog. 10th ed. New York: The H. W. Wilson Company, 1961.

(Supplements through 1960.) Provides an author, title, and subject index to a selected list of books for children, with descriptive comment; also evaluates.

Cumulative Book Index. Includes books published in the field of education in the English language.

The Education Index. New York: The H. W. Wilson Company, 1929–   . Indexes educational periodicals, books, pamphlets, monographs, and reports of the United States and Great Britain by author and subject; monthly issues include check lists of the latest publications in the field of education.

The Educational Film Guide. New York: The H. W. Wilson Company, 1954–1958 volume. (Annual supplements.) A title listing of 16mm motion-picture films on all subjects for classroom and nontheatrical use; indicates grade level; provides a subject index to the titles listed.

Filmstrip Guide. 11th ed. New York: The H. W. Wilson Company, 1953. *Supplement.* 1955–1958. Lists filmstrips on all subjects available free, or for purchase, rent, or free loan.

Strang, Ruth, and Others. *Gateways to Readable Books.* 3d ed. New York: The H. W. Wilson Company, 1958. An annotated list of books in many fields for adolescents who find reading difficult (subtitle).

Standard Catalog for High School Libraries. 7th ed. New York: The H. W. Wilson Company, 1957. (Annual supplements.) Lists and evaluates books for junior and senior high school libraries.

————. 7th ed. with *Catholic Supplement.* Contains, in addition to the books listed in the regular edition, 643 books, 73 pamphlets, and 24 magazines selected especially for Catholic high schools by the Catholic Library Association.

Dictionaries and Encyclopedias

Good, Carter Victor (ed.). *Dictionary of Education.* New York: McGraw-Hill Book Company, Inc., 1959. Defines and explains professional terms in education and related fields.

Harris, Chester W., and Liba, Marie R. (eds.). *Encyclopedia of Educational Research.* 3d ed. New York: The Macmillan Company, 1960. Gives the status of research in all phases of education and includes articles on methods of research and the characteristics of particular groups, such as the gifted and the retarded.

Monroe, Paul (ed.). *A Cyclopedia of Education.* New York: The Macmillan Company, 1911. 5 vols. Presents all aspects of education as a science and as an art; is especially valuable for history and philosophy of education.

Rivlin, Harry N. (ed.). *Encyclopedia of Modern Education.* New York: The Philosophical Library, Inc., 1943. Gives a summary of present achievements in education; explains problems of present-day education for lay people as well as for professional workers.

Handbooks

Feingold, Leonard, and Feingold, Lillian. *Scholarships, Fellowships, and Loans.* Cambridge, Mass.: Bollman Publishing Company, 1949–1955. 3 vols.

Handbook of Private Schools. 41st ed. Boston: Porter Sargent, Publisher, 1960.

International Handbook of Universities. Paris, International Association of Universities, 1959– . Supplies general information about universities in seventy-one foreign countries.

Junior Colleges and Specialized Colleges. Boston: Porter Sargent, Publisher, 1960.

UNESCO. *Study Abroad.* New York: International Documents Service, Columbia University Press, 1948– . (Annual.)

Biographical Dictionaries and Directories

American Council on Education. *American Junior Colleges.* 5th ed. Washington, D.C.: American Council on Education, 1960. Provides information on junior colleges in the United States, the Canal Zone, Guam, and Puerto Rico.

————. *American Universities and Colleges.* 8th ed. Washington, D.C.: American Council on Education, 1960. Gives detailed information about accredited institutions of higher education in the United States.

Cattell, Jacques. (ed.). *Directory of American Scholars.* New York: R. R. Bowker Company, 1942, 1951, 1957. Vol. I and vol. II include scholars in the humanities and the social sciences; vol. II includes college and university administrators and professors and members of learned societies.

————, and Ross, E. E. (eds.). *Leaders in Education.* 3d ed. Lancaster, Pa.: The Science Press, 1948. Includes teachers, administrators, and research workers in education.

Patterson's American Education. Chicago: Educational Directories, Inc., 1904– . (From 1904 through 1953 carried the title *Patterson's Ameri-*

can Educational Directory.) Includes a classified directory of schools, libraries, educational systems of the states and their officers.

U.S. Office of Education. *Education Directory*. Washington, D.C.: Government Printing Office. 1912–   . (Annual.) Lists Federal, state, county, city, and higher education officers and officers of educational associations.

Who's Who in American Education. Nashville, Tenn.: Who's Who in American Education, Inc., 1928–   . (Biennial.) Gives a cross section of the field of education in the United States and Canada.

Examples of Professional Journals in Education

Childhood Education. 1924–   . (Monthly except June to August.)

Educational Leadership. 1945–   . (Monthly except June to September.)

Elementary School Journal. 1900–   . (Monthly except June to August.)

Journal of Educational Psychology. 1910–   . (Monthly except June to September.)

Catholic Educational Review. 1911–   . (Monthly except June to August.)

CHAPTER NINETEEN

LANGUAGE (PHILOLOGY)

PHILOLOGY (by derivation, the love of learning and the love of speech and discourse) is that branch of learning concerned with human speech and what it reveals about man.

Language as a subject was first studied because it was important in reading and in understanding literature, and emphasis was placed upon the study of Greek, Latin, and Hebrew, since most of the early writing was done in those languages. When the study of language, as such, emerged as a branch of learning during the nineteenth century, it was called linguistics.

Linguistics, the scientific study of human speech, includes an investigation of the sound, form, and meaning of language and of the relations of one language to another.

The study of language as a branch of knowledge includes:

1   Morphology, the study of the historical development of speech patterns

2   Syntax, the study of the use and forms of the language and of the parts of speech and their various forms
3   Etymology, the study of the origin of words
4   Semantics, the historical and psychological study of meaning and change of meaning of words

In the study of language and linguistics, dictionaries are the major aids, both the general word dictionaries of a language and dictionaries which provide more than a mere listing of the words of a language and their several meanings. The latter include:

1   Dictionaries based on the historical development of words
2   Etymological dictionaries
3   Dictionaries of usage
4   Dictionaries of slang, dialect, and colloquialisms
5   Dictionaries of synonyms and antonyms
6   Dictionaries of pronunciation

Other types of reference books useful in the study of language are bibliographies, indexes, general histories of language, and biographical dictionaries.

USEFUL REFERENCE BOOKS IN LANGUAGE
Bibliographies and Indexes[1]

Collison, Robert Lewis. *Dictionaries of Foreign Languages.* New York: Hafner Publishing Company, 1955. Provides historical and explanatory notes about the general and technical dictionaries of the chief foreign languages.

Education Index. Includes educational publications in the field of language.

International Index. Indexes periodicals in the field of language and linguistics.

Dictionaries of Language as a Subject Field

Pei, Mario, and Gaynor, Frank (eds.). *A Dictionary of Linguistics.* New York: Philosophical Library, Inc., 1954. Presents the more frequently used

[1] See also Chapter Thirteen, Bibliographies.

terminology in the field of historical linguistics, some more modern terminology, grammatical terms, and brief descriptions of the major dialects of the world.

Dictionaries of Certain Aspects of Language

ETYMOLOGY[2]

Partridge, Eric (ed.). *Origins.* 2d ed. New York: The Macmillan Company, 1959. Emphasizes civilization rather than science; includes the most common words in modern English.

HISTORICAL DEVELOPMENT OF WORDS

Craigie, Sir William, and Hulbert, James R. (eds.). *A Dictionary of American English on Historical Principles.* 2d ed. Chicago: University of Chicago Press, 1960. 4 vols. Indicates words which originated in America or which are in greater use here than elsewhere and words which are important in the history of America; follows the plan of the *Oxford English Dictionary.*

Murray, Sir James Augustus Henry, and Others (eds.). *The Oxford English Dictionary.* London: Oxford University Press, 1933. 12 vols. and supplement. Presents the historical development of each word which has entered the English language since 1150.

PRONUNCIATION

Kenyon, John S., and Knott, Thomas A. (eds.). *A Pronouncing Dictionary of American English.* Springfield, Mass.: G. & C. Merriam Company, 1953. Gives pronunciation only, according to the alphabet of the International Phonetic Association.

SLANG, DIALECT, COLLOQUIALISMS

Berrey, Lester V., and Van Den Bark, Melvin (eds.). *The American Thesaurus of Slang.* 2d ed. New York: Thomas Y. Crowell Company, 1953. A collection of colloquialisms, slang, and vulgarisms arranged according to the ideas which they express; has an alphabetical word index for ease of use.

Mathews, Mitford N. (ed.). *A Dictionary of Americanisms on Historical Principles.* Chicago: University of Chicago Press, 1956. Includes words which have been added to the English language in the United States from colonial times to the present.

---

[2] In etymological dictionaries, definitions as such are not given. The meaning of the word is determined through the etymology.

Wentworth, Harold, and Flexner, Stuart B. (eds.). *Dictionary of American Slang*. New York: Thomas Y. Crowell Company, 1960. Provides etymology, quotations, and cross references.

SYNONYMS AND ANTONYMS

Roget's International Thesaurus. New ed. revised. New York: Thomas Y. Crowell Company, 1946. Groups words according to the ideas which they express, making use of the index essential.

The New American Roget's College Thesaurus in Dictionary Form. New York: Grosset & Dunlap, Inc., 1958. Follows the traditional dictionary arrangement.

Webster's Dictionary of Synonyms. Springfield, Mass.: G. & C. Merriam Company, 1942. Distinguishes between words of like meaning by discrimination and illustration.

USAGE

Evans, Bergen, and Evans, Cornelia (eds.). *A Dictionary of Contemporary American Usage*. New York: Random House, Inc., 1957. Covers current English in the United States, emphasizing current good usage.

Fowler, Henry Watson (ed.). *A Dictionary of Modern English Usage*. London: Oxford University Press, 1940. Arranged alphabetically by topic, explains how to write and how not to write; explains usage of words and phrases.

FOREIGN WORDS AND PHRASES[3]

Mawson, C. O. Sylvester (comp.). *Dictionary of Foreign Terms*. New York: Thomas Y. Crowell Company, 1934. Includes proverbs, mottoes, and quotations from more than fifty foreign languages found in English and American writings; indicates language derivations.

Newmark, Maxim (comp.). *Dictionary of Foreign Words and Phrases*. New York: Philosophical Library, Inc., 1950. Emphasizes current usage; provides English equivalents or definitions of foreign terms which have become part of our contemporary English vocabulary.

Biographical Dictionaries[4]

Directory of American Scholars. Includes living persons in the field of language.

[3] See also Chapter Seven, Dictionaries.
[4] See also Chapter Ten, Biographical Dictionaries.

Histories of Language

Baugh, Albert C. *A History of the English Language.* Revised ed. New York: Appleton-Century-Crofts, Inc., 1957.

Bloomfield, Leonard. *Language.* New York: Henry Holt and Company, 1946.

Graff, William L. *Language and Linguistics.* New York: Appleton-Century-Crofts, Inc., 1932.

Hayakawa, S. I. *Language in Thought and Action.* Revised ed. New York: Harcourt, Brace and Company, Inc., 1949.

Jespersen, Otto. *Language: Its Nature, Development, and Origin.* New York: The Macmillan Company, 1922.

Pei, Mario. *The Story of Language.* Philadelphia: J. B. Lippincott Company, 1949.

Vendryes, J. *Language: A Linguistic Introduction to History.* New York: Alfred A. Knopf, Inc., 1925.

Professional Journals

American Speech. 1925–   . (Quarterly.)

Modern Language Association of America. *Publications.* 1884–   . (Five times a year.)

Modern Language Notes. 1886–   . (Monthly except July to October.)

Studies in Philology. 1906–   . (Quarterly.)

CHAPTER TWENTY

THE SCIENCES

THE word "science," deriving from the Latin word which means to learn or to know, is, in its broadest sense, synonymous with learning and knowledge, and in general usage, it means an organized body of knowledge. In a more restricted meaning, science is organized knowledge of natural phenomena and of the relations between them.

The 500 class of the Dewey Decimal System is assigned to Pure Science, and includes mathematics, astronomy, physics, chemistry, anthropology, geology, biology, botany, and zoology. Applied Science (technology) is placed in the 600 class, which comprises the medical sciences, engineering, agriculture, home economics, business, chemical technology, manufactures, and building construction.

Books on the sciences are out of date more quickly than those in any other subject field, and the student who seeks material on a topic in any of these areas must consult periodicals, abstract journals, and original sources—such as papers read at scientific meetings, reports, and patent applications—for the latest information. In addition to these sources, there are reference books designed to provide answers to the many questions which arise in this broad subject area. Among the most useful kinds of reference books are bibliographies and guides, professional journals, abstract journals,[1] indexes, handbooks, dictionaries and glossaries (both English and foreign language), encyclopedias, yearbooks, directories, biographical dictionaries, and general histories.[2]

The importance of frequently consulting the bibliographies in periodicals and abstract journals and the library card catalog in order to keep up with new materials in this rapidly changing field cannot be overemphasized.

USEFUL REFERENCE BOOKS IN THE SCIENCES

Bibliographies and Guides[3]

Crane, Evan Jay, and Others. *A Guide to the Literature of Chemistry*. 2d ed. New York: John Wiley & Sons, Inc., 1957. Gives procedure for literature searching and methods of keeping up-to-date on the literature of the field; comprehensive in coverage.

Cumulative Book Index. New York: The H. W. Wilson Company, 1898–   . Indexes by subject and author books in print in the English language in the sciences.

Hawkins, Reginald Robert (ed.). *Scientific, Medical and Technical Books Published in the United States of America*. 2d ed. New York: R. R. Bowker Company, 1958. Describes selected titles in science, medicine, and technology.

Mellon, Melvin Guy. *Chemical Publications*. 3d ed. New York: McGraw-Hill Book Company, Inc., 1958. Surveys all kinds of chemical publications and explains ways of using them advantageously.

[1] An abstract journal lists and provides digests or summaries of periodical articles and other literature. Abstracts may be in the original language in which the article appeared, or they may be translated into English or another language.
[2] See pp. 138–140 for a discussion of these kinds of reference books and the purposes they serve.
[3] See also Chapter Thirteen, Bibliographies.

Parke, Nathan Grier. *Guide to the Literature of Mathematics and Physics.*
2d revised ed. New York: Dover Publications, 1958. Includes
works in related fields; emphasizes the usefulness of each kind of reference material; gives points on the use of the library and on finding
material on a subject.

Indexes

The Agricultural Index. New York: The H. W. Wilson Company, 1916–   .
A subject guide to publications in agricultural and allied fields; covers
periodicals, pamphlets, bulletins, and reports.
Applied Science and Technology Index. New York: The H. W. Wilson
Company, 1958–   . (Monthly except August.) One of two indexes
which replaced *Industrial Arts Index;* indexes by subject periodicals in
aeronautics, automation, physics, chemistry, engineering, industrial and
mechanical arts, and related fields.
Education Index. 1929–   . Indexes educational publications in the sciences.
Engineering Index. 1906–   . New York: Engineering Index, Inc., 1934–   .
(Annual.) Continues the *Engineering Index* begun in 1884; has a
classed subject index: civil engineering, electrical engineering, etc.
Industrial Arts Index. New York: The H. W. Wilson Company, 1913–1957.
A subject index to periodicals in the fields of business, science, and
technology; was divided into two separate indexes—*Applied Science
and Technology Index* and *Business Periodicals Index*—in January,
1958.
Readers' Guide to Periodical Literature. 1900–   . Indexes nontechnical
scientific periodicals.

Dictionaries

Besserer, C. W., and Besserer, Hazel (comps.). *Guide to the Space Age.*
Englewood Cliffs, N.J.: Prentice-Hall, Inc., 1960. Defines terms in the
field of space technology and allied fields; uses non-technical language
whenever possible.
Chambers's Technical Dictionary. Edited by C. F. Tweney and L. E. C.
Hughes. 3d ed. revised, with supplement. New York: The Macmillan
Company, 1958. Defines and explains terms in automation, nuclear
physics, and electronics.
DeVries, Louis (ed.). *German-English Science Dictionary.* 3d ed. New York:

McGraw-Hill Book Company, Inc., 1959. For students in physics, chemistry, biology, agriculture, and related sciences; has a supplement of new terms.

Gray, H. J. (ed.). *Dictionary of Physics.* New York: Longmans, Green & Co., Inc., 1958. Provides some bibliographies and biography.

Hinsie, Leland E., and Shatzky, Jacob (eds.). *Psychiatric Dictionary.* 3d ed. (Oxford Medical Series.) New York: Oxford University Press, 1960. Gives pronunciation, illustrations, and quotations.

James, Glenn, and James, Robert C. (eds.). *Mathematics Dictionary.* 2d ed. Princeton, N.J.: D. Van Nostrand Company, Inc., 1959. For students, engineers, and others using mathematics in their profession; gives exhaustive coverage of terms; has multilingual index.

Spitz, Armand, and Gaynor, Frank. *A Dictionary of Astronomy and Astronautics.* New York: Philosophical Library, Inc., 1959. Provides answers to technical questions in these fields.

Stedman's Medical Dictionary. 19th ed. Baltimore: The Williams & Wilkins Company, 1957. Gives derivation and pronunciation of words; has illustrations and biographical sketches.

Encyclopedias

Clark, George L., and Hawley, G. G. (eds.). *The Encyclopedia of Chemistry.* New York: Reinhold Publishing Corporation, 1957. *Supplement.* 1958. Gives an overview of the field; has signed articles.

Clark, Randolph L. J., and Cumley, Russell W. (eds.). *The Book of Health.* New York: Elsevier Press, Inc., 1953. A medical encyclopedia for everyone (subtitle). Presents the body of medical knowledge at the present time.

The McGraw-Hill Encyclopedia of Science and Technology. New York: McGraw-Hill Book Company, Inc., 1960. 15 vols. Covers the fields of life science, physical science, earth science, and engineering; provides concise basic information on any scientific or technological subject; has detailed index; includes bibliographies.

Rudaux, Lucien, and Vaucouleurs, Gerard de (eds.). *Larousse Encyclopedia of Astronomy.* New York: Prometheus Press, 1959. Devoted entirely to the science of space; presents the basic foundations of astronomy.

Van Nostrand's Scientific Encyclopedia. 3d ed. Princeton, N.J.: D. Van Nostrand Company, Inc., 1958. Provides a comprehensive reference library of the major sciences and fields of technology.

Handbooks

Handbook of Chemistry and Physics. Cleveland, Ohio: Chemical Rubber
   Publishing Company, 1914–   . A ready-reference book of chemical and
   physical data (subtitle).
Jordan, E. L. *Hammond's Nature Atlas of America.* New York: C. S. Ham-
   mond & Co., Inc., 1952. Designed for nature lovers who are not
   scientists; provides illustrations and text.
"Putnam's Nature Field Books." New York: G. P. Putnam's Sons, 1928–   .
   This series includes separate volumes on specific scientific subjects.
   Titles include *Field Book of American Wild Flowers,* by F. S. Mathews;
   Field Book of the Stars, by W. T. Olcott; and *Field Book of Common
   Rocks and Minerals,* by F. B. Loomis.
Urquhart, Leonard Church. *Civil Engineering Handbook.* 4th ed. New
   York: McGraw-Hill Book Company, Inc., 1959. Gives principles,
   methods, data; covers main divisions of civil engineering.

Yearbooks

The American Yearbook. 1929–   . Gives summaries of progress in the
   sciences.
U.S. Department of Agriculture. *Yearbook of Agriculture.* Washington, D.C.:
   Government Printing Office, 1894–   . Covers a specific subject in each
   issue.
U.S. Department of Interior, Bureau of Mines. *Minerals Yearbook.* Washington, D.C.: Government Printing Office, 1933–   . Reviews performance
   and developments in the nation's mineral industries; includes statistical
   summaries.

Biographical Dictionaries[4]

Cattell, Jaques (ed.). *American Men of Science.* 9th ed. Vol. I: *The Physical
   Sciences.* (Living persons.) Vol. II: *The Biological Sciences.* (Living
   persons.) Vol. III: *The Social and Behavioral Sciences.* (Includes living
   persons in anthropology.) New York: R. R. Bowker Company, 1956.
Directory of American Scholars.
Howard, A. V. (ed.). *Chambers's Dictionary of Scientists.* New York: E. P.
   Dutton & Co., Inc., 1952. Universal in coverage; includes scientists
   from earliest times to the present.

[4] See also Chapter Ten, Biographical Dictionaries.

Leaders in American Education.

Leaders in American Science. Nashville, Tenn.: Who's Who in American Education, Inc., 1953–1959. (Biennial.) Gives sketches of the lives of eminent living persons in industrial, governmental, educational areas of the sciences; covers the United States and Canada.

Professional Journals

American Journal of Physics. 1933–   . (Monthly except June to August.)

Journal of Chemical Education. 1924–   . (Monthly.)

Mathematics Teacher. 1908–   . (Monthly except June to September.)

Natural History. 1900–   . (Monthly except July to August.)

Science. 1883–   . (Weekly.)

Sky and Telescope. 1941–   . (Monthly.)

Abstract Journals

Biological Abstracts. 1926–   . (Monthly; semimonthly in December.)

Chemical Abstracts. 1907–   . (Semimonthly.)

Mathematical Reviews. 1940–   . (Monthly except August.)

CHAPTER TWENTY-ONE

THE FINE ARTS

ART, from the Latin *ars,* is any skill or aptitude which enables its possessor to perform in a superior manner. This meaning of the word covers (1) the fine arts, which express ideas, emotions, and experiences in beautiful or significant forms; (2) the useful arts, which are both utilitarian and artistic; (3) the decorative arts, which adorn rather than create; and (4) the recreational arts, which afford relaxation and amusement.

The fine arts, as a branch of knowledge, are those arts (skills or aptitudes) concerned with creating, producing, or expressing what is beautiful, imaginative, or appealing for its own sake, rather than for some utilitarian purpose. Traditionally, the fine arts include music, painting, sculpture, dance, drama, architecture, and poetry.

In the Fine Arts class of the Dewey Decimal System (700), all of the above-named fine arts are included except poetry. Landscape and civic arts, drawing and decorative arts, prints and print making, photography, and recreation are also placed in the 700 Class.

Works of art, that is, paintings, sculpture, musical scores, dramatic productions, etc., constitute the primary source materials in the fine arts subject field. There are, however, many reference books designed to aid the student in understanding and appreciating works of art; the artists who produced them; the technical terminology of the several areas; the historical backgrounds of schools, movements, and trends; and the actual techniques employed. These reference aids include bibliographies, guides and catalogs, indexes to periodical literature and to paintings and illustrations, dictionaries and encyclopedias, biographical dictionaries, handbooks, histories, and professional journals.[1]

USEFUL REFERENCE BOOKS IN THE FINE ARTS

Bibliographies, Guides, and Indexes

The Art Index. New York: The H. W. Wilson Company, 1929– . (Quarterly.) Indexes art journals and museum publications by author and subject; includes both fine arts and applied arts.

Baker, Blanche M. *Theatre and Allied Arts.* New York: The H. W. Wilson Company, 1952. Lists more than 6,000 historical, biographical, technical, and cultural works; provides annotations.

Chamberlin, Mary. *Guide to Art Reference Books.* Chicago: American Library Association, 1959. Evaluates the literature of art.

Logasa, Hanna. *Index to One-act Plays, 1900–1924.* Boston: F. W. Faxon Company, 1924. Four supplements cover the period from 1924 to 1957. Indexes one-act plays in collections by title, author, and subject.

Monro, Isabel S., and Monro, Kate M. *Index to Reproductions of American Paintings.* New York: The H. W. Wilson Company, 1948. Lists by name of artist, by title, and sometimes by subject the reproductions of American paintings in more than 800 books.

———, and ———. *Index to Reproductions of European Paintings.* New York: The H. W. Wilson Company, 1956.

———, and ———. *Costume Index Supplement.* New York: The H. W. Wilson Company, 1956. Indexes by subject, illustrations and text in

---

[1] See pp. 138–140 for a discussion of these kinds of reference books and the purposes they serve.

347 books which have appeared since the publication of *Costume Index* in 1937.

Dictionaries and Encyclopedias

Adeline's Art Dictionary. Translated from the French and enlarged. New York: D. Appleton-Century Company. Inc., 1910. Gives brief, clear definitions and explanations; many illustrations.

Apel, Willi. *Harvard Dictionary of Music*. Cambridge, Mass.: Harvard University Press, 1956. Provides a comprehensive list of definitions, articles on techincal bibliographies, and short musical illustrations.

Dictionary of Modern Ballet. New York: Tudor Publishing Company, 1959. Presents a complete record of the modern dance from Diaghilev and Isadora Duncan to the present day.

Encyclopedia of World Art. New York: McGraw-Hill Book Company, Inc., 1959– . 15 vols. (In progress.) Includes biographies of artists, monographic treatments of periods, movements, and areas of art; discussions of types, media, technology, concepts, and problems of art.

Encyclopedia of Painting. Edited by Bernard S. Myers. New York: Crown Publishers, Inc., 1955. Gives a factual and critical account of painters and painting of the world from prehistoric times to the present; addressed to the student and the general public.

Ewen, David. *Encyclopedia of Concert Music*. New York: Hill and Wang, Inc., 1959. Companion volume to *Encyclopedia of the Opera;* covers best known compositions in all branches of instrumental music, past and present, excluding semiclassical and "pop" music.

————. *Ewen's Musical Masterworks*. 2d ed. New York: Arco Publishing Company, 1954. Gives brief discussions of thousands of musical works in every field of music, arranged alphabetically by composer; includes summaries of plots of operas and evaluations of composers and works.

Feather, Leonard G. *Encyclopedia of Jazz*. New York: Horizon Press, 1955. Includes history, biography, glossary of terms, bibliography, and guide to recordings.

The Focal Encyclopedia of Photography. New York: The Macmillan Company, 1956. Gives the techniques, the art, and the business of photography.

Grove's Dictionary of Music and Musicians. 5th ed. Edited by Eric Blom. London: Macmillan & Co., Ltd., 1954. 9 vols. Includes periodical articles; gives bibliography and a classified arrangement of composers' works; covers all phases of the field of music (supplement, 1961).

Menke, Frank G. *The Encyclopedia of Sports.* New and revised ed. New York: A. S. Barnes and Company, 1953. Includes information about the background and rules of sports and about the participants.

The Praeger Picture Encyclopedia of Art. New York: Frederick A. Praeger, Inc., 1958. Surveys painting, sculpture, architecture, and other arts from the earliest times to the present.

Scholes, Percy A. *The Concise Oxford Dictionary of Music.* New York: Oxford University Press, 1957. An abridgment of his *Oxford Companion to Music,* gives brief information on composers, musical compositions, performances, and terminology.

Thompson, Oscar (ed.). *The International Cyclopedia of Music and Musicians.* 8th ed. Revised by Nicolas Slonimsky. New York: Dodd, Mead, & Company, Inc., 1959. Provides definitions, bibliography, biography, synopses of opera plots, pronunciation of the names of musicians.

Handbooks

Ewen, David. (ed.). *Complete Book of the American Musical Theater.* New York: Henry Holt and Company, Inc., 1958. Includes plots, production history, stars, songs, composers, librettists, and lyricists of more than 300 productions since 1886.

————. *Complete Book of 20th Century Music.* 2d ed. Englewood Cliffs, N.J., Prentice-Hall, Inc., 1959.

Hartnoll, Phyllis (ed.). *The Oxford Companion to the Theatre.* 2d ed. New York: Oxford University Press, 1957. Emphasizes the popular rather than the literary theater in all countries; gives history of the theater in the United States in detail.

Reinach, Salomon. *Apollo.* New York: Charles Scribner's Sons, 1935. An illustrated manual of the history of art throughout the ages (subtitle).

Biographical Dictionaries

American Art Annual. Washington, D.C.: American Federation of Arts, 1898–   . Provides current directory and institutional information.

Ewen, David (ed.). *American Composers Today.* New York: The H. W. Wilson Company, 1949.

————. *European Composers Today.* New York: The H. W. Wilson Company, 1954.

————. *Living Musicians.* New York: The H. W. Wilson Company, 1940. *First Supplement.* 1957. Lists the most important works of each composer with biographical information; includes portraits.

Directory of American Scholars. 1st ed.

Who's Who in American Art. New York: R. R. Bowker Company, 1937–   .
    Gives biographies of American and Canadian artists, a list of open exhibitions, and a geographical index.

Professional Journals

American Artist. 1937–   . (Monthly, September to June.)

Musical America. 1898–   . (Sixteen numbers.)

The Musical Quarterly. 1915–   .

Journal of Health-Physical Education-Recreation. 1930–   . (Monthly except May to August.)

School Arts. 1901–   . (Monthly except July and August.)

CHAPTER TWENTY-TWO

LITERATURE

ANY discussion of reference books in the field of literature must be prefaced by a definition and a delimiting of the term literature.

In its broadest sense, literature includes all preserved writings. In a more limited but still general denotation, it is the total written works of a people, such as the literature of America or the literature of England. It is also the name given to all writings upon a particular subject, such as the literature of geography, the literature of education, or the literature of history.

Specifically and as a subject area, literature is that class of writing which is notable for imaginative and artistic qualities, form, or expression. The forms of literature are poetry, drama, prose fiction, and essay.

Reference books in the field of literature are more numerous than in any other subject field. There are reference books which cover all forms of literature, and there are reference books in each of the literary genres, such as poetry, drama, and fiction.

Since each reference book is designed to serve a particular purpose, the representative books listed below are grouped according to the purposes they serve and the kinds of questions they answer. Distinguishing features of each book are noted with the bibliographical entry.

BIBLIOGRAPHIES AND GUIDES

Bibliographies and guides in literature, as in other areas of knowledge, are designed to locate, describe, and evaluate the literature of the field. They may group works according to form, such as poetry, drama, fiction, essays; they may be complete and include all works; or they may be selective, listing only a part of the literature. Not all bibliographies and guides do all these things.

Baker, Ernest A., and Packman, James (eds.). *A Guide to the Best Fiction, English and American.* New and enlarged ed. New York: The Macmillan Company, 1932. Describes the contents, nature, and style of each book listed; has author, title, and subject index.

Bateson, F. W. (ed.). *The Cambridge Bibliography of English Literature.* New York: Cambridge University Press, 1941. 4 vols. *Supplement: A.D. 600–1900.* Edited by George Watson. New York: Cambridge University Press, 1957. Arranged chronologically by literary group and literary form, the four-volume work and the supplement provide a complete bibliography of all writings in book form, English and Latin, of interest to the British Empire up to 1955; evaluates.

Blanck, Jacob (comp.). *Bibliography of American Literature.* New Haven: Yale University Press, 1955–1959. 3 vols. A selective bibliography limited to the past 150 years of American literature; describes but does not evaluate.

Dickinson, Asa Don. *The World's Best Books.* New York: The H. W. Wilson Company, 1953. Includes books during the period from 1050 B.C. to A.D. 1950.

The Fiction Catalog. New York: The H. W. Wilson Company, 1950. *Supplement.* 1951–1955; 1956–1958; 1960. Lists works of fiction by author, title, and subject; has annotations; indicates books especially suitable for young people.

Literary History of the United States. Edited by R. E. Spiller and others. New

York: The Macmillan Company, 1948. 3 vols. Vol. III is bibliography; classifies literature by author, period, and literary type; describes and evaluates.

————. *Bibliography Supplement.* Edited by Richard M. Ludwig. New York: The Macmillan Company, 1959.

INDEXES

An index in the field of literature locates an article in a periodical or locates a poem, quotation, fairy story, play, essay, or other work in an anthology. Since the person seeking information does not always know the title and the author of the poem, play, or essay he needs, a means of locating these items by subject is also necessary. It may be necessary to locate quotations by means of key words. The following indexes provide some or all of these kinds of listings; they are representative of the indexes available.

Book Review Digest. 1905–   . Includes a subject and title index to the books listed in each volume.

Brewton, John E., and Brewton, Sara W. (comps.). *Index to Children's Poetry.* New York: The H. W. Wilson Company, 1942. *First Supplement.* 1954. Indexes by subject, author, title, and first line the poetry in selected collections for children and young people.

Cook, Dorothy E., and Monro, Isabel W. (comps.). *Short Story Index.* New York: The H. W. Wilson Company, 1953. *Short Story Index Supplement, 1950–1954.* 1956. *Short Story Index Supplement, 1955–1958.* 1960. Lists entries under author, title, and subject.

Eastman, Mary Huse (comp.). *Index to Fairy Tales, Myths, and Legends.* 2d ed. revised and enlarged. Boston: The F. W. Faxon Company, 1926. *First Supplement.* 1937. *Second Supplement.* 1952. Indexes by title or key words of title, by subject, and by racial and geographical categories.

Essay and General Literature Index, 1900–1933. New York: The H. W. Wilson Company, 1934. (Supplements, 1934–1954; semiannual supplements, 1954–   .) Indexes books and parts of books by author and subject and by title when necessary.

Granger's Index to Poetry and Recitations. 3d ed. revised and enlarged. Chicago: A. C. McClurg & Company, 1940. Indexes both standard and popular collections of poetry and prose recitations by title, author, and first line.

Granger's Index to Poetry. 4th ed. completely revised and enlarged. New York: Columbia University Press, 1953. *Supplement to Fourth Edition.* 1957. (The fourth edition and supplement do not include prose selections.) Indexes anthologies of poetry published to December, 1955, by title, first line, and subject.

Ottemiller, John H. (comp.). *Index to Plays in Collections.* 3d ed. revised and enlarged. New York: Scarecrow Press, 1957. Includes, by author and title, plays appearing in collections published between 1900 and 1956.

Sell, Violet, and Others (comps.). *Subject Index to Poetry for Children and Young People.* Chicago: American Library Association, 1957. Indexes by form as well as by subject.

West, Dorothy Herbert, and Peake, Dorothy M. (comps.). *Play Index, 1949–1952.* New York: The H. W. Wilson Company, 1953. Covers plays of all kinds by author, title, subject, and number and kind of cast; includes annotations.

DICTIONARIES AND ENCYCLOPEDIAS

Dictionaries and encyclopedias of literature define words and phrases; identify references to fictional, mythical, and legendary places, characters, and events; explain the historical, geographical, social, economic, and cultural backgrounds of literature; provide biographical and critical information about authors and their works; and in some cases give pronunciation, summaries or plots, and bibliographical references. Some useful dictionaries and encyclopedias of literature follow.

Brewer's Dictionary of Phrase and Fable. Revised and enlarged ed. New York: Harper & Brothers, 1953. Defines, identifies, and explains phrases and allusions in nonfiction, folklore, and legend; gives pronunciation; is universal in scope.

Cassell's Encyclopaedia of Literature. Edited by S. H. Steinberg. New York: Funk & Wagnalls Company, 1953. 2 vols. Covers all forms of literature; gives definitions, background material, brief summaries of plots, bibliography; includes biographical information on authors from the earliest times to date.

Columbia Dictionary of Modern European Literature. Edited by Horatio

Smith. New York: Columbia University Press, 1947. Limited to Continental Europe of the twentieth century and immediately preceding; provides biography, bibliography, and evaluative comment.

Newmark, Maxim (comp.). *Dictionary of Spanish Literature.* New York: Philosophical Library, Inc., 1956. Covers the literature found in textbooks for the teaching of Spanish; evaluates, defines, and summarizes plots; provides biography and background material.

Richards, Robert Fulton (ed.). *Concise Dictionary of American Literature.* New York: Philosophical Library, Inc., 1955. Points out what is important in American literature; evaluates.

Shipley, Joseph T. (ed.). *Dictionary of World Literature.* New York: Philosophical Library, Inc., 1943. Emphasizes criticism, forms, techniques; does not give summaries of works or biographical information.

———. *Encyclopedia of Literature.* New York: Philosophical Library, Inc., 1946. 2 vols. Presents surveys of the literatures of the world, both major and minor.

HANDBOOKS

Handbooks provide short, concise answers to questions about literary terminology, works, trends, and movements affecting literature and about events, places, and characters referred to in literature. The Oxford Companion series, which is listed below, provides this kind of information, although each volume in the series may vary in points of emphasis. The other handbooks listed immediately following the Oxford Companions provide some or all the types of information listed above.

Hart, James D. (ed.). *The Oxford Companion to American Literature.* 3d ed. New York: Oxford University Press, 1956. Presents the American mind and the American scene as they are reflected in and influenced by American literature.

Harvey, Sir Paul (ed.). *The Oxford Companion to English Literature.* 3d ed. New York: Oxford University Press, 1946. Emphasizes English authors, literary works, and movements of present or of historical importance.

———. *The Oxford Companion to Classical Literature.* New York: Oxford University Press, 1937. Provides information about classical allusions found in all literature; gives biographical and background material.

————, and Heseltine, Janet E. (eds.). *The Oxford Companion to French Literature*. New York: Oxford University Press, 1959. Surveys French literary life from the emergence of the vernacular to 1939.

Barnhart, Clarence L., and Halsey, William D. (eds.). *The New Century Handbook of English Literature*. New York: Appleton-Century-Crofts, Inc., 1956. Addressed to laymen; places emphasis on English writers and works; gives pronunciation.

Benét, William Rose (ed.). *The Reader's Encyclopedia*. New York: Thomas Y. Crowell Company, 1955. An encyclopedia of world literature and the arts; covers trends, movements, allusions, plots, characters in fiction, mythology, legend, biography, current and slang terms.

Johnson, Burges (comp.). *New Rhyming Dictionary and Poet's Handbook*. Revised ed. New York: Harper & Brothers 1957. Groups words that rhyme; characterizes words as colloquial, slang, pedantic.

The Reader's Companion to World Literature. New York: The Dryden Press, Inc., 1956. Provides material on authors, works, types of literature, terminology, myths, periods, and movements.

Thrall, William Flint, and Hibbard, Addison (eds.). *A Handbook to Literature*. Revised and enlarged by C. Hugh Holman. New York: The Odyssey Press, Inc., 1960. Explains words, phrases, movements peculiar to literary study; includes an outline of the literary history of England and America.

LITERATURE IN COLLECTIONS (ANTHOLOGIES)

Book Digests

Keller, Helen Rex. *The Reader's Digest of Books*. New and greatly enlarged. New York: The Macmillan Company, 1929. Gives brief digests of books, arranged alphabetically by author.

Magill, Frank N. (ed.). *Masterplots*. New York: Salem Press, Inc., 1955. First series, 3 vols. *Annual volume*, 1954. Each digest is preceded by a listing of the type of work, the author, type and time of plot, locale, date of first publication, and principal characters.

————. *Masterpieces of World Literature in Digest Form*. Third series. New York: Harper & Brothers, 1960. First series, 1952. Second series, 1956. Comparable to *Masterplots* in arrangement; the third series emphasizes poetry and philosophical works; has some essay-type reviews; is universal in scope.

Anthologies of Poetry

Oxford Book of American Verse. Chosen and edited by Bliss Carmen. London: Oxford University Press, 1928.

Oxford Book of American Verse. Edited by F. O. Matthiesen. New York: Oxford University Press, 1950.

Oxford Book of English Verse, 1250–1918. New ed. Chosen and edited by Arthur Quiller-Couch. New York: Oxford University Press, 1939.

Oxford Book of French Verse. Chosen by St. John Lucas. London: Oxford University Press, 1926.

Oxford Book of Irish Verse. Edited by Donagh McDonagh. London: Oxford University Press, 1958.

Stevenson, Burton Egbert (comp.). *The Home Book of Verse, American and English*. 9th ed. New York: Henry Holt and Company, Inc., 1953.

———. *Home Book of Modern Verse*. 2d ed. New York: Henry Holt and Company, Inc., 1953.

BOOKS OF QUOTATIONS

Books of quotations provide (1) quotations on a subject for speeches or papers and (2) the correct wording and source of a given quotation. There are many collections of quotations; each one includes some quotations omitted in others, and thus they supplement each other. The usefulness of a book of quotations depends on (1) the kind of quotations included, (2) the kind of reference provided (name of author, work from which the quotation is taken, collection in which it can be located, with page, stanza, or line), and (3) the ways each quotation is indexed (author, title, subject, first line, key word). Some useful collections of quotations are listed below.

Bartlett, John (ed.). *Familiar Quotations*. 13th ed.; completely revised. Boston: Little, Brown & Company, 1955. Presents quotations which are "familiar or worthy of being familiar"; has author, subject, and key-word indexes.

The Oxford Dictionary of Quotations. 2d ed. New York: Oxford University Press, 1953. Includes quotations based on popularity, not on merit; has an index of key words.

Stevenson, Burton Egbert (ed.). *Home Book of Quotations.* 9th ed. New York: Dodd, Mead & Company, Inc., 1959. Emphasizes American political quotations, campaign slogans, catch lines from popular songs; includes both classical and modern selections.

Taylor, Archer, and Whiting, Bartlett J. (comps.). *A Dictionary of American Proverbs and Proverbial Phrases, 1820–1880.* Cambridge, Mass.: The Belknap Press of Harvard University, 1958. Arranges quotations in chronological order; has bibliography.

Walsh, William Shepard (ed.). *International Encyclopedia of Prose and Poetical Quotations.* Revised ed. Philadelphia: John C. Winston Company, 1951. Provides a complete concordance to the quotations included; emphasizes quotations from the writings and speeches of contemporary writers and statesmen.

BIOGRAPHICAL DICTIONARIES

General encyclopedias, biographical dictionaries, handbooks, and histories of literature provide much information on the lives and works of authors. In addition to these sources, there are biographical dictionaries which are devoted exclusively to authors.

Kunitz, Stanley J., and Haycraft, Howard (eds.). *The Junior Book of Authors.* New York: The H. W. Wilson Company, 1934. Covers the lives of writers and illustrators of books for young readers from Lewis Carroll and Louisa M. Alcott to the present time.

———, and ———. *British Authors before 1800.* New York: The H. W. Wilson Company, 1952.

———, and ———. *British Authors of the Nineteenth Century.* New York: The H. W. Wilson Company, 1936.

———, and ———. *American Authors, 1600–1900.* New York: The H. W. Wilson Company, 1938.

———, and ———. *Twentieth Century Authors.* New York: The H. W. Wilson Company, 1942.

Kunitz, Stanley J. (ed.). *Twentieth Century Authors: First Supplement.*

New York: The H. W. Wilson Company, 1955. The biographical information in this authors series, edited by Kunitz and Haycraft, includes lists of works, bibliographies, and portraits of the authors included.

Hoehn, Matthew. *Catholic Authors*. Newark, N.J.: St. Mary's Abbey, 1948. Gives lengthy sketches of Catholic authors of the period 1930 to 1947.

Magill, Frank N. (comp.). *Cyclopedia of World Authors*. New York: Harper & Brothers, 1958. Contains biographical sketches of those authors whose works are included in *Masterpieces of World Literature in Digest Form*.

Cattell, Jacques (ed.). *Directory of American Scholars*. 3d ed. New York: R. R. Bowker Company, 1957. Includes persons in literature and language.

REFERENCE HISTORIES AND CRITICISM

The Cambridge History of English Literature. London: Cambridge University Press, 1907–1927. 15 vols. Emphasizes movements in English literature, influence of foreign literature on the literature of England, and bibliographies.

The Cambridge History of American Literature. New York: G. P. Putnam's Sons, 1917–1921. 4 vols. Gives trends, evaluation, and extensive bibliographies.

The Oxford History of English Literature. New York: Oxford University Press, 1947– . 12 vols. (In progress.) Each volume or half volume will be an independent book; the twelve volumes will provide a continuous and comprehensive history of English literature; includes bibliographies.

Moulton, Charles Wells (ed.). *The Library of Literary Criticism of English and American Authors*. Buffalo: Moulton Publishing Company, 1901–1905. 8 vols. (Reprinted in 1934 by Peter Smith, New York.) Chronologically arranged by authors; includes both obscure and prominent writers; is a compilation of materials by numerous authors.

Nyren, Dorothy (ed.). *A Library of Literary Criticism*. New York: Frederick Ungar Publishing Co., 1960. A collection of literary criticism from scholarly journals and books covering American authors who became prominent after 1900; includes a selective list of books by the author under consideration.

PROFESSIONAL AND LITERARY JOURNALS

American Literature. 1929–   . (Quarterly.)
College English. 1939–   . (Monthly.)
English Journal. 1912–   . (Monthly except July and August.)
Poetry. 1912–   . (Monthly.)
Saturday Review. 1924–   . (Weekly.)

USING THE LIBRARY
FOR A RESEARCH PAPER

PART FIVE

USING THE LIBRARY
FOR A RESEARCH PAPER

CHAPTER TWENTY-THREE

THE UNDERGRADUATE
RESEARCH PAPER

THE word "research" means search, inquiry, pursuit, and it comes from the French word *rechercher*, which means to seek again.

The true research paper involves not only studious inquiry into a subject, but also critical and exhaustive investigation of that subject for the purpose of revising accepted conclusions concerning it in the light of facts uncovered by the investigation.

It may be said that elementary research begins when the first encyclopedia the student consults fails to provide the information which he needs to answer a question or to carry out an assignment, and he is forced to consult several sources.

In general, the college research paper (on the undergraduate level) is an exposition designed to present, not evaluate, the results of the student's inquiry into, or investigation of, a chosen subject.

The undergraduate-level research paper—sometimes called a *term paper*—may be one of several kinds.

1   It may be a report which relates facts for the purpose of informing the reader or of showing progress over a period of time.

2   It may be a report, based on the student's investigations, which analyzes an event, a situation, or a period.

3   It may be a thesis,[1] that is, a paper which states and maintains by argument a position or a proposition.

4   It may be a thesis taking the form of presentation and evaluation of facts for the purpose of persuading or recommending.

The successful completion of any research paper depends upon the careful investigation of a subject; the ability to choose and evaluate materials and to take clear, well-documented notes; an understanding of the purpose and forms of footnotes and bibliography; and clear, logical, and orderly development and presentation of facts in keeping with the purpose of the paper.

PROCEDURE

Some of the basic steps in writing a research paper are listed below.

1   Select a subject. In making the choice of a topic, consider these factors:

    a   Is this a subject of sufficient interest to you that you can make it interesting to your readers?

    b   Can you study it seriously in the length of time allotted for writing the paper?

    c   Can you cover it adequately in the number of words prescribed by your instructor?

    d   Is it likely that you will find sufficient material on it to write a paper, or is it too new, too highly specialized, or too limited in appeal to have received coverage in books, newspapers, or magazines?

2   Restrict your subject if the topic you have chosen is too broad or too general for the assigned paper.

---

[1] Thesis is also the name given to a dissertation presented by a candidate for an academic degree, usually the M.A. or M.S. degree.

a   Look in the card catalog under your subject and read the subject headings immediately following to see how that subject is subdivided. Notice the subject headings listed at the bottom of each card to find further subdivisions and related headings. For example, if your general topic is "books," you may find in the card catalog:

Books   Books—Printing—History
Books—Advertising   Books—Psychology
Books—Format   Books—Statistics
Books—History   Books, Talking
Books—Microphotographic
    reproductions

b   Find your subject in a periodical index and notice the subdivisions. For example,[2]

Books   Books—Conservation and
Books—Care   restoration
Books—Censorship   Books, Talking
   See Censorship   *See* Phonograph records
                                     —Books

c   See how a general encyclopedia subdivides your subject.

d   You may restrict your topic according to period of time or geographical location or according to historical, social, cultural, or political significance; for example:

Printers and Printing in Colonial America
The Political Influence of the Printer in Colonial America
The Cultural Significance of the Invention of Printing
The Economic Background of the Medieval Universities
The Book in the 1960s

In the following list of subjects, notice the progression from general to specific:

The Story of Books and Libraries
Books and Libraries—Antiquity

<hr>

[2] From: *Readers' Guide to Periodical Literature* (New York: The H. W. Wilson Company, March, 1955–February, 1956), p. 165.

Books and Libraries—Antiquity—Assyria
Books and Libraries—Antiquity—Assyria—669–626 B.C.

3   Choose the phase of your subject that you wish to investigate.
4   Decide upon the purpose of your paper.

   a   Is it to inform?
   b   Is it to show progress?
   c   Is it to analyze an event, a situation, or a period?
   d   Is it to persuade and recommend?

5   Make a tentative statement of your thesis, that is, of the proposition you will attempt to defend, clarify, or develop. For example, "The institution of monasticism was of major importance in the preservation and development of literature during the Middle Ages," or "the printing press hastened the era of discovery and exploration."

   a   Analyze your thesis as to the subject areas it includes or touches: geography, sociology, economics, history, literature, politics.

   b   Decide what kinds of sources will provide the information you will need to write your paper.

      (*1*)   Primary sources[3]—interviews, questionnaires, letters, diaries, manuscripts, memoirs

      (*2*)   Secondary sources—books, journals, encyclopedias, and other reference books

   c   Determine the chronological period in which your subject falls.

6   Begin your preliminary search for material. In the preceding chapters, reference sources have been discussed, with emphasis upon their usefulness in providing material on a subject. Since subject headings are the key to the card catalog, the indexes, and to most reference books, it is necessary, before using any of these sources, to determine the headings under which your subject may be listed.

   a   Consult the card catalog to find the books in your library in which your subject, or any relevant phase of it, is discussed. Read the entire card carefully to see what the book covers, the amount and kind of illustrative material it includes, the bibliographical references provided, the number of topics treated, and the topic

---

[3] Primary sources are those materials which have not been interpreted by another person. Secondary sources are materials which have been reported, analyzed, or interpreted by other persons.

which is given the greatest emphasis. (The first subject heading listed is the subject which is given the widest coverage.) Study the subject headings as an indication of other subjects which will lead to material on your subject. For example, if your subject is "The Book in the 1960s," some of the headings under which you will find material are;

Books
Books—Format
Books—History—Twentieth century
Books—Statistics
Books, Talking

Libraries—History
Microfilm books
Microcards
Paperback books
Printing—History

b Take the class number or numbers, and browse in these sections of the stacks, looking at the tables of contents and the indexes of books which may be helpful.

c Consult a printed bibliography or guide to see what material has been written on your subject which may not be listed in the card catalog, such as parts of books, pamphlets, and reports.

d Use a general dictionary for general definitions; use a subject dictionary for specialized definitions and terminology.

e Find an overview of your topic in a general encyclopedia, and then consult a subject encyclopedia for technical and specialized information.

f Use general and subject indexes to find recent material in periodicals and to find selections in collected works.

g Consult a handbook for statistical information or for identification of allusions to persons, events, dates, and legendary or mythological figures.

h Look up important persons connected with your subject in a biographical dictionary.

i Establish geographical locations and facts with the aid of an atlas or a gazetteer.

j Use primary sources whenever possible.

It is essential that you use a variety of sources in order to obtain a broad view of your subject; to see it in its various phases; to discover the factors which influenced or contributed to it; to know the individuals, groups, or organizations associated with it; to become acquainted with current thinking as well as with past opinion regarding it; and to have some understanding of the terminology of the field in question.

7   Begin preliminary reading.

   a   Read a background or overview article in a textbook or in a history of the subject.

   b   Examine a general article in an encyclopedia.

   c   Read a popular article in a periodical.

   d   Skim through the material at first.

   e   Make brief notes of references for later serious reading, giving adequate information for finding these references easily.

8   As you examine material, make a tentative bibliography of the materials which you think you will use.

   a   Make the bibliography on cards.

      (*1*)   Use cards of uniform size.

      (*2*)   Use a separate card for each bibliographical reference.

   b   Give basic information for each reference.

      (*1*)   Author

      (*2*)   Title

Figure 14   Sample bibliography card.

```
                                              Ref
                                              912
                                              Sh4h
        Shepherd, William R.
        Historical Atlas.  8th ed.   New York:
        Barnes & Noble, Inc., 1956.

            Has map of Phoenicia, p. 6.
```

(3) Facts of publication

(4) Page or pages on which information can be found

c Include a brief descriptive statement of each work, indicating the content and/or the usefulness for your subject.

9 Make a tentative outline of the major divisions of your paper. An outline of the major divisions of Chapter One, A Brief History of Books and Libraries, is as follows:

I. Introduction

II. Thesis: The story of books and libraries, from earliest times to the present, is primarily the story of systems of writing, the forms of the written documents, and the methods of preserving them and of making them accessible for use.

III. Primitive means of communication

IV. Writing, books, and libraries

A. Antiquity

1. The Sumerians, Babylonians, and Assyrians

2. The Egyptians

3. Other Semitic peoples

4. The Chinese

5. The Greeks

6. The Romans

B. The Middle Ages

1. The monasteries

2. The universities

3. Printing with movable types

C. The Modern Era

1. 1500–1900

2. The twentieth century

10 Begin serious reading.

11 Take notes.

a The kinds of notes you may take include:

(1) A restatement, in your own words, of the thought or thoughts of an author. It is important that in your paraphrase you do not lose the meaning of the original statement when you take it out of context.

(2) A direct quotation, copied exactly, including punctuation.

Durant, Will   901
Our Oriental Heritage   D93s
V.I. The Story of Civilization
New York: Simon and Schuster, 1942
p. 106

  The Phoenicians were not the originators
of the alphabet; they imported it from Egypt
and Crete, then exported it, along with
their other wares, to all of the cities along
the Mediterranean.

Ezekiel XXVII, 33.   Revised Standard
                            Version

  When your wares came from the
    seas,
   you [Tyre] satisfied many peoples;
with your abundant wealth and
    merchandise
  you enriched the kings of the earth.

Lissner, Ivar   901
The Living Past   L691
Tr. from the German by J. M. Brownjohn
New York: G. P. Putnam's Sons, 1957
pp. 95-100

  Brief but comprehensive coverage of the
Phoenicians: the people, their geographical
location, their activities as traders and
manufacturers, their religion, their cities,
their contributions as "transmitters of
culture."

       Very useful

*Figure 15   Sample note cards: (top) restatement or paraphrase, (center) quotation,
(bottom) evaluative comment.*

Any omission must be indicated by an ellipsis (. . .); any interpolation must be indicated by brackets.

(3)   A critical or evaluative comment about a book or a person.

b   Use cards for your notes.

(1)   Use cards of uniform size throughout.

(2)   Give complete bibliographical information on the first card for each reference:

(a)   Author's full name

(b)   Complete title

(c)   Imprint: place of publication, publisher, date

(d)   Pages and volume

(e)   Month, day, year, volume, and pages of periodical articles

(f)   Month, day, year, and pages of newspaper articles

c   Use one card for each reference. If more than one card is required to complete a note, number all cards and put the author's last name on all cards after the first.

d   Leave space at the top of the card for the subject headings, which will be the subdivisions of your outline.

12   Formulate your thesis.

a   State it simply, expressing the basic idea which you will develop.

b   Restrict it to one approach to the subject.

c   Avoid using ambiguous words or phrases.

13   Study your notes in order to restrict your subject further.

14   Make a preliminary detailed outline, either topical or in sentence form. Whatever form you choose, use it throughout your outline.

a   Make sure that your outline is organized in a logical manner, that each division and subdivision receives proper emphasis, and that each part of the outline is in the appropriate relationship to other parts of the outline.[4]

b   Fill in the gaps in your outline by additional reading and note-taking.

c   Discard irrelevant material.

[4] Show the relationship of subdivisions in an outline (or of items in an enumeration) by indentation and the use of letters and numerals in the following order: I, A, B, 1, a, b, (1), (a), (b), (i).

15 Remake your outline.
16 Write the first draft of your paper.
17 Use footnotes when necessary.
    a Give the source of a direct quotation.
    b Acknowledge the source of an opinion or a discussion which you have paraphrased or of any specific material which cannot be considered common knowledge.
    c Give credit for statistical information, graphs, and charts you have used.
    d Suggest additional reading on a particular point.
    e Add an explanation to clarify or expand a statement in the text of your paper.
    f Make cross references to other parts of your paper.
18 Make a bibliography.
    a Give the sources of the materials which you have used in writing the paper.
    b Suggest additional reading materials.
    c Include an entry for each work mentioned in a footnote.
19 Revise your paper.
20 Evaluate the entire paper, as to clarity of purpose, proper emphasis of important ideas and divisions, elimination of gaps and irrelevant material, accuracy in presenting or in interpreting facts, appropriateness of the choice of words, correctness of grammatical structure and form, unity and coherence in writing, adequacy of documentation, and consistency of bibliographical and footnote form.
21 Write the final draft of your paper.

FOOTNOTES AND BIBLIOGRAPHY

Footnotes give the exact location of the sources of certain kinds of information used in the text of the research paper; bibliography describes, as a whole, the work or works from which the citations are taken. The forms for footnotes and bibliography—that is, the order of listing the items and the punctuation, capitalization, and underlining of words in the title—

vary according to the manual of style[5] which is followed by a college or by a department within a college. Each department may adopt a different form. In general, the variations are not in the items included but in the style in which they are presented. Footnote and bibliographical forms are not the same, and entries for books, periodical and newspaper articles, encyclopedia articles, and for special materials differ from each other.

Before writing a research paper, a student must understand the forms which he is required to use in making footnotes and bibliography, and he must follow those prescribed forms consistently.

FOOTNOTES

In general, footnotes are numbered consecutively and are placed at the bottom of the page, in numerical order, separated from the text by a solid line across the page. However, all footnotes may be placed at the end of the paper in a section for notes.

Arabic numerals are used as footnote reference indexes, but asterisks and other symbols may be used also. Whatever reference symbol is employed, it must follow the passage to which it refers and must be placed after it (following the punctuation mark if there is one), just above the line.

The first citation of a footnote reference must give complete information in logical order.

1   Author's name (usually not inverted)
2   Title of publication
3   Facts of publication: place, publisher, and date
4   Volume and page numbers
5   Date of periodicals

Listed below are examples of one of the forms which may be used in making footnotes.

[1] Charles H. Haskins, *The Rise of Universities* (Ithaca, N.Y.: Great Seal Books, 1957), p. 10.

[5] Two manuals of style are Kate L. Turabian, *A Manual for Writers of Term Papers, Theses, and Dissertations* (Chicago: University of Chicago Press, 1955) and William Giles Campbell, *Form and Style in Thesis Writing* (Boston: Houghton Mifflin Company, 1954).

[2] William C. Hayes, "Daily Life in Ancient Egypt," *The National Geographic Magazine,* LXXX (October, 1941), 419–515.

[3] "Phoenicia," *The Encyclopedia Americana,* XXI (1958), 786–788.

[4] Arthur Haseloff, "Illuminated Manuscripts," *Encyclopaedia Britannica,* 14th ed., XII, 95–100.

Usually the complete form of a reference is not repeated after it is first given; a shortened form is used, as follows:

1   When references to the same work follow each other without any other reference in between, use the abbreviation, *ibid.,* from the Latin word, *ibidem,* meaning in the same place.

[1] Louis B. Wright, *The Cultural Life of the American Colonies, 1607–1763* (New York: Harper & Brothers, 1957), p. 70.

[2] *Ibid.* (*Ibid.* is used in place of the full reference and indicates that the source is exactly the same.)

[3] *Ibid.,* p. 87. (In this case, *ibid.* replaces everything except the page number.)

2   An abbreviation may be used in place of the title after a reference has been cited fully, unless there has been more than one reference by the same author. The shortened form would include the author's last name and the abbreviation *op. cit.,* which comes from *opere citato,* meaning in the work cited.

[1] Charles H. Haskins, *The Rise of Universities* (Ithaca, N.Y.: Great Seal Books, 1957), p. 10.

[2] James W. Thompson, *The Medieval Library* (New York: Hafner Publishing Company, 1957), p. 49.

[3] Haskins, *op. cit.,* p. 40.

BIBLIOGRAPHY[6]

There is no single correct form for making a bibliography, but there are several principles which must be adhered to in any form which is followed:

[6] See Chapter Thirteen for a discussion of bibliography.

1   All bibliographical entries must be in accord with the purpose of the research paper.
2   All items must be presented accurately, clearly, and logically.
3   The bibliographical form which is prescribed for a given paper must be followed consistently in every entry.

The following items are included in a bibliographical entry:

1   The name of the author
2   The title of the book as it appears on the title page
3   The edition, if it is other than the first
4   The number of volumes in the set, if the entire set is used
5   The place of publication, name of publisher, and date of publication
6   The number of pages in the book and the price, if these items are required by the instructor.

Bibliographical entries may be grouped according to kind—books, newspapers, periodicals—or according to the main divisions in the research paper. They are arranged alphabetically within the groups.

Some examples of one form for making a bibliography are given below.

Books

ONE AUTHOR

Haskins, Charles H. *The Rise of Universities*. Ithaca, N.Y.: Great Seal Books, 1957.

TWO AUTHORS

Arnett, L. D., and Arnett, Esther T. *Readings in Library Methods*. New York: G. E. Stechert & Company, 1931.

SEVERAL AUTHORS

Dutcher, George Matthew, *et al.* [or Dutcher, George Matthew, and Others]. *Guide to Historical Literature*. New York: The Macmillan Company, 1931.

AN ORGANIZATION OR INSTITUTION AS AUTHOR

American Council on Education. *American Universities and Colleges*. 8th ed. Washington, D. C.: American Council on Education, 1960.

U.S. Bureau of the Census. *Statistical Abstract of the United States.* Washington, D.C.: Government Printing Office, 1960.

AN EDITION OF AN AUTHOR'S WORK

Kenyon, Frederic George. *Books and Readers in Ancient Greece and Rome.* 2d ed. New York: Oxford University Press, 1951.

AN AUTHOR'S WORK EDITED BY ANOTHER PERSON

Chiera, Edward. *They Wrote on Clay: The Babylonian Tablets Speak Today.* Edited by George G. Cameron. Chicago: University of Chicago Press, 1938.

A TRANSLATION

Herodotus. *The History of Herodotus.* Translated by George Rawlinson. New York: Tudor Publishing Company, 1951.

AN EDITED COLLECTION

Walsh, William Shepard (ed.). *International Encyclopedia of Prose and Poetical Quotations.* Revised ed. Philadelphia: John C. Winston Company, 1951.

A VOLUME IN A SERIES

Mellon, Melvin Guy. *Chemical Publications.* 3d ed. (International Chemical Series.) New York: McGraw-Hill Book Company, Inc., 1958.

Articles

ENCYCLOPEDIA—SIGNED AND UNSIGNED

Haseloff, Arthur. "Illuminated Manuscripts," *Encyclopaedia Britannica,* 14th ed., XII, 95–100.
"Phoenicia," *The Encyclopedia Americana,* XXI (1958), 786–788.

PERIODICAL

Hayes, William C. "Daily Life in Ancient Egypt," *The National Geographic Magazine,* LXXX (October, 1941), 419–515.

AN ESSAY IN A COLLECTED WORK

Waller, Robert. "Mass Media," *Arts, Artists, and Thinkers,* ed. John Murray Todd. New York: Longmans, Green & Co., Inc., 1958.

NEWSPAPER

Jonas, Jack. "A Visit to a Land of Many Facets," *The Sunday Star* (Washington, D.C.), March 5, 1961, sec. F, p. 1.

Unpublished Material

Arkansas Library Commission. "Statistics for County and Regional Libraries." Little Rock: Arkansas Library Commission, 1949. (Typewritten.)

※ APPENDIX ※

SOME ABBREVIATIONS IN COMMON USE AND TABLES

SOME ABBREVIATIONS
IN COMMON USE

anon. Anonymous

bibl. Bibliography

c., ca. About (*circa*)

cf. Compare

comp. Compiler, compiled

ed. Edition, editor, edited

e.g. For example (*exempli gratia*)

enl. Enlarged

et al. And others

fig. Figure

ff. Following

fl., flor. Flourished (*floruit*)

front. Frontispiece

ibid. In the same place (*ibidem*)

i.e. That is (*id est*)

illus. Illustrations, illustrator, illustrated

imprint On a catalog card or in a bibliographic entry, the place, publisher, and date of publication

infra. Below (to be mentioned later) (*infra*)

loc. cit. In the place cited (*loco citato*)

ms. (mss.) Manuscript (manuscripts)

n.d. No date of publication in imprint

op. cit. In the work cited (*opere citato*)

pam. Pamphlet

passim. Throughout; here and there

pl. Plate, plates

p., pp. Page, pages

pseud. Pseudonym

q.v. Which see (*quod vide*)

sb. Substantive

sup., supp., suppl. Supplement

supra Above (previously mentioned) (*supra*)

tr., trans. Translated, translator

viz. To wit, namely (*videlicet*)

vol. Volume

	SCOPE	VOCABULARY INCLUDES	TREATMENT OF WORDS	OTHER FEATURES
Funk & Wagnalls New Standard	All live words in the English language; dialects spoken by large numbers of English-speaking people	Standard, technical, scientific, dialect words; biographical, geographical, mythological, and Biblical names	Spelling, pronunciation, part of speech, inflectional forms, etymology; definitions in reverse chronological order, synonyms, antonyms, derivatives	Illustrations, illustrative quotations from newspapers, periodicals; appendices: foreign words, disputed spellings, simplified spelling rules, statistics of population
Oxford English Dictionary	All words now in use in English or in use since 1150	Standard, obsolete, colloquial words; technical words English in form; dialect before 1500	Spelling, pronunciation, part of speech, inflectional forms, etymology; usage, definitions in historical order, synonyms, derivatives	Date each word entered the language with illustrative quotation for each use
Webster's New International Dictionary (2d ed.)	All literary and most of technical and scientific vocabulary of modern English beginning ca. 1500	Standard, technical, scientific, obsolete, slang, dialect, foreign words; proverbs; proper names, names in fiction	Spelling, pronunciation, part of speech, inflectional forms, etymology; definitions in historical order, synonyms explained, antonyms, derivatives	Illustrations, illustrative quotations from literature, divided page; "new words" section; appendices: abbreviations, signs, and symbols, pronouncing gazetteer, biographical section
American College Dictionary	Selection of most frequently used words and of scientific and technical words	Standard, technical, scientific, obsolete, foreign words; proper names; abbreviations	Spelling, pronunciation, part of speech, inflectional forms, etymology; variant spelling; definitions in reverse chronological order, synonyms, antonyms, derivatives	Usage guide, signs and symbols, given names
Webster's Collegiate	Selected vocabulary to meet needs of college students and general reader	Standard, technical, scientific words; limited selection of slang, dialect, obsolete, foreign words; proper names	Spelling, pronunciation, part of speech, inflectional forms, etymology; definitions in historical order, synonyms explained, antonymns, derivatives	Appendices: abbreviations, signs and symbols, gazetteer, rhymes, orthography, biography, punctuation, list of colleges and universities

A COMPARATIVE ANALYSIS OF SELECTED GENERAL ENCYCLOPEDIAS

	LEVEL	SPECIAL AIDS	STRONG POINTS
Americana	Educated adult	Bibliography after article, cross references, topical index, maps in text, pronunciation, signed articles	Science, technology, evaluation of literary and artistic works, texts of historical documents, information on United States towns, cities, states, history of each century
Britannica	Educated adult	Bibliography after article, cross references, detailed and comprehensive index, maps (in atlas volume), signed articles	Science, applied science, medicine, pre-twentieth century art, "covers subjects in depth"
Collier's	Junior college, high school, general public	Bibliography (in last volume—by subject, not by article), cross references, index, maps in text, pronunciation, signed articles	All modern subjects, popular style
Compton's	High school, upper elementary grades	Bibliography after article, cross references, fact-index in each volume, maps and other visual aids in text, pronunciation, list of contributors	Broad subject-area articles, study outlines with many articles, fact-index, readability, illustrative material
World Book	High school, children, home	Graded bibliography with some annotations after articles, cross references, maps and other visual aids in text, signed articles	Readability (written for age and grade levels), reading and study guide, illustrations, orderly, simple style, study outlines
Columbia	Office, home, general public	Brief bibliography after article, cross references, pronunciation	Brevity, United States towns, obscure people, place names

FEATURES OF SELECTED GENERAL INDEXES

	INDEXED FROM	FREQUENCY OF ISSUE	METHOD OF INDEXING	EXTENT OF INDEXING	SPECIAL AIDS
Bibliographic Index	1938	Semimonthly	Subject	Bibliographies only: those published as books and pamphlets, those appearing in books, pamphlets, and periodical articles, including some foreign periodicals	List of periodicals indexed, cross references, explanation of sample entry, key to abbreviations
Biography Index	1946	Quarterly	Subject	Biographies only: those in periodicals indexed in Wilson indexes, in current books of individual and collective biography in the English language, obituaries of important persons in periodicals and the *New York Times*	List of periodicals indexed, cross references, key to abbreviation, index by profession, explanation of sample entry
Book Review Digest	1905	Monthly	Author of book reviewed, subject, title	Book reviews only, in about seventy English and American periodicals	List of periodicals indexed, explanation of entry, length of review, cumulative five-year indexes
Catholic Periodical Index	1930	Quarterly	Author, subject	Complete indexing of selected Catholic periodicals; notes many articles written from Catholic viewpoint elsewhere	List of periodicals indexed, key to abbreviations, explanation of entry
Essay and General Literature Index	1900	Semiannually	Author, subject, distinctive title	Essays and articles in collections of essays and collections of miscellaneous works, biography, criticism, book reviews	Lists of books indexed, directions for use, key to abbreviations
Readers' Guide to Periodical Literature	1900	Semimonthly	Author, subject, title when necessary	Articles, poems, plays, fiction, films in about 100 general and non-technical periodicals	List of periodicals indexed, cross references, explanation of entry, key to abbreviations
New York Times Index	1913	Semimonthly	Subject	Articles, book reviews, essays, poems, biographies in *New York Times*	Cross references, synopses of some articles

FEATURES OF SELECTED SUBJECT INDEXES

	INDEXED FROM	FREQUENCY OF ISSUE	METHOD OF INDEXING	EXTENT OF INDEXING	SPECIAL AIDS
Agricultural Index	1916	Monthly	Subject	More than 115 periodicals in agriculture and allied fields, agricultural books, bulletins, pamphlets, reports, USDA and state experiment station reports, book reviews	List of periodicals indexed, key to abbreviations, explanation of entry, cross references, lists of new books
Applied Science and Technology Index	1958	Monthly	Subject	About 200 periodicals in pure science, applied science, and related fields	List of periodicals indexed, key to abbreviations, explanation of entry, cross references
Art Index	1929	Quarterly	Subject, author	More than 100 periodicals in fine and applied arts, American and foreign, museum bulletins and annuals; covers book reviews, notices of exhibitions; illustrations, reproductions of paintings	List of periodicals indexed, key to abbreviations, explanation of entry, cross references
Business Periodicals Index	1958	Monthly	Subject	Index to periodicals in business, trade, and related fields	List of periodicals indexed, key to abbreviations, explanation of entry, cross references
Education Index	1929	Monthly	Author, subject	More than 120 educational periodicals in the United States and Great Britain, yearbooks, pamphlets, books, society transactions, parts of books; book reviews under that heading	List of periodicals indexed, key to abbreviations, explanation of entry, classified check lists of professional publications and government publications
International Index	1907	Quarterly	Author, subject	About 170 of the more scholarly journals, including some foreign, in the social sciences and humanities	List of periodicals indexed, key to abbreviations, explanation of entry, cross references

FEATURES OF SELECTED BIOGRAPHICAL DICTIONARIES

	SCOPE	COVERAGE	KIND OF INFORMATION PROVIDED	SPECIAL AIDS
Current Biography	Universal	Living persons in the news	Long articles; personal data, evaluative comments from other sources, publications, portrait	Pronunciation of unusual names, bibliography, index by profession
Cyclopedia of Names	Universal	Persons living and not living	Brief personal data	Pronunciation
Dictionary of American Biography	United States	Persons not living who have made some significant contribution to American life	Scholarly, authoritative articles; personal data, evaluative comments, bibliographies	Index volume, signed articles
Dictionary of National Biography	Great Britain	Persons not living who have achieved some distinction in any walk of life	Long, scholarly, objective articles; personal data, background material, evaluative comment	Index, bibliographies, signed articles
International Who's Who	Universal	Living persons of international standing in all fields	Very brief articles; personal data, positions held, publications	Address of biographee
National Cyclopaedia of American Biography	United States	Persons living and not living who have contributed to history	Lengthy articles; personal data, background, some illustrations	Index
Webster's Biographical Dictionary	Universal	Noteworthy persons living and not living	Concise personal data	Pronunciation
Who's Who	Great Britain	Living persons of prominence	Brief personal data; position, education, publications	
Who's Who in America	United States	Living persons in all lines of useful and reputable achievement	Brief personal data; positions, education, publications	Pronunciation beginning vol. 22
World Biography	Universal	Living persons important in any field	Detailed personal data; gives profession, not publications	

FEATURES OF SELECTED BIOGRAPHICAL DICTIONARIES IN A SUBJECT FIELD

	SCOPE	COVERAGE	KIND OF INFORMATION PROVIDED	FIELD
American Men of Science	United States	Living persons	Brief personal data, memberships, publications, scientific interests	Scientists, pure and applied; 9th ed., vol. 3, includes social science, psychology, geography
Catholic Authors	Universal	Persons living and not living	Personal data, list of works	Catholic professional writers
Cyclopedia of World Authors	Universal	Persons living and not living	Critical and biographical data, publications, bibliographical references	Authors covered in Masterpieces of World Literature and Masterplots
Dictionary of Scientists	Universal	Persons living and not living	Brief personal data, major achievements, publications	History of science
Directory of American Scholars	United States	Living persons	Brief personal data, position, publications, memberships	Scholars in the humanities and social sciences, administrators and professors in higher education
Encyclopaedia of Literature	Universal	Persons living and not living	Personal data, evaluative comment, publications, bibliographical references to critical and biographical material	Professional authors (literature)
Grove's Dictionary of Music and Musicians	Universal	Persons living and not living	Lengthy articles; personal data, publications or compositions, evaluative comment	Musicians, composers, artists
Junior Book of Authors	Universal	Persons living and not living	Lengthy articles; personal data, evaluative comment, publications	Authors and illustrators of children's books
Psychological Register, vols. 2, 3	Universal	Living persons	Brief personal data, publications, bibliographies	Psychologists
Twentieth Century Authors	Universal	Persons living and not living	Lengthy articles; personal data, evaluative comments, list of works by and about, portrait	Professional authors (literature)
Who's Who in American Education	United States	Living persons	Brief personal data, positions, memberships, publications	Educators, all areas
Who's Who in Art	Universal	Living persons	Brief personal data	Artists, teachers, designers, critics, writers, collectors

INDEX

NOTES

NOTES

NOTES

NOTES

NOTES

NOTES

NOTES

NOTES